Fiction as Knowledge

Fiction as Knowledge

The Modern

Post-Romantic

Novel

John McCormick

with a new introduction
by the author

Transaction Publishers
New Brunswick (U.S.A.) and London (U.K.)

New material this edition copyright © 1999 by Transaction Publishers, New Brunswick, New Jersey.
Originally published in 1975 by Rutgers University Press, New Brunswick, N.J.

This book is printed on acid-free paper that meets the American National Standard for Permanence of Paper for Printed Library Materials.

Library of Congress Catalog Number: 98–34564
ISBN: 0–7658–0480–8
Printed in the United States of America

Library of Congress Cataloging-in-Publication Data
McCormick, John, 1918–
    Fiction as knowledge : the modern post-romantic novel / John McCormick ; with a new introduction by the author.
        p.   cm.
    Originally published: New Brunswick : Rutgers University Press, 1975
    Includes bibliographical references and index.
    ISBN 0–7658–0480–8 (alk. paper)
    1. Fiction—20th century—History and criticism. I. Title.
PN3503.M23   1998
809.3—dc21   98–34564
                                                                          CIP

For Mairi

Acknowledgments

As ever, I owe a large but unspecified debt to my students, without whose interest and discussion much of what follows would be less than lucid. I am grateful to the Rutgers University Research Council for time and opportunity in which to read and write. My debt to Joseph Frank of Princeton University is greater than I can briefly acknowledge; his example as man and as scholar has sustained me over a period of many years. I thank the advisory committee of the Christian Gauss Seminars in literary criticism, Princeton University, for its invitation to deliver as lectures portions of the book in hand.

J. McC.

Contents

Introduction to the Transaction Edition

In his review of a light-hearted study of ancient Greek plea-
sures, the Regius Professor of Greek at Oxford remarks that "Literature . . . often disappoints the sober historian; it suffers from
rhetoric, ignorance and imagination" (Peter Parsons, "Eels Tomorrow, but Sprats Today." Review of James Davidson, *Courtesans
and Fishcakes: The Consuming Passions of Classical Athens* [Lon-
don: HarperCollins (sic),1997]. *London Review of Books*, xix, no.
18, 18 September 1997, 6). Such a view strikes me as perverse and
as wrong as a fine scholar can be, but the sentiment, with respect
to fiction in particular, proposes exactly what I set out to rectify,
many years ago, in writing *Fiction as Knowledge*, and in giving
the work that title. Rectifiers famously come to grief: see among
others J.J. Rousseau, K. Marx, Neville Chamberlain, Richard
Nixon. I still hope not to have joined so eminent a company in my
efforts, however.

Some would say that although the recent "sober historian" is
likely to substitute graphs for rhetoric, he often suffers from ignorance and want of imagination. Unsober (drunken) historians from
the eighteenth century to the recent past relied on documentary
evidence whenever possible, but the merit of their histories lay in
their use both of documents and of literature, all of which provided an imaginative grasp of the "truth" of times past. The most
enduring historians, I believe, realized early on that truth is an ideal
rather than a reality to be grasped and reproduced in their writings.
Our vogue of "contemporary history" has produced people who
are doomed to wade through vast, newly available archives, trivial

or vital e-mail records which they "access," and all the works and pomps of the internet, but one must doubt that their record of the truth is any more reliable as history than Gibbons's, Macaulay's or Henry Adams's imaginative rhetoric. Henry Adams's novel, *Democracy*, I suggest, contains as much or more "truth" than his nine-volume *History of the United States during the Administrations of Jefferson and Madison*.

Every period has its peculiarities: one of ours is that history, like poetry, is read only by other historians, as poetry seems to be read mainly by poets. The reasons are myriad, but prominent among them is Literary Theory, a literary theory based upon a vulgarization of German phenomenology by French and United States theorists, in which the past becomes a bad joke to be derided and ignored. It is a movement that attracts because it substitutes the easily acquired jargon of deconstruction for knowledge, and it often results in cynicism disguised as philosophical skepticism. That sad development was only beginning when I wrote the introduction of 1975. Now, apparently, it is triumphant, but signs are appearing to indicate that some at least of the traditional approaches in the arts are beginning to flourish; not least, a growing awareness of the impossibility of self-invention, and of the intellectual aridity that results from historical ignorance or half-informed defiance.

I should like to think that the easy jargon of deconstruction justifies one thesis of *Fiction as Knowledge*: that for all its conflicting labels, literature since the high summer of romanticism has remained "romantic" in that the subjective insight of the writer dominated any other approach for a very long time. As I read it, deconstruction, which purports to kill off romantic subjectivism, is in itself an egregious display of romantic subjectivism. From Paris to New Haven to Berkeley, California, we have been instructed to disregard the writer for the word, the syllable, as interpreted in the arcane diction of none other than the critic. In the theology of high romanticism, it was the artist, and supreme among artists, the poet whose genius gave him perceptions divorced from classical and neoclassical aesthetics. The poet, the artist, was the Creator; his interpreters humble followers, disciples, or devil's advocates whose work was by definition partial and directed not to eternity but only to the passing day. The academic deconstructionist, however, has displaced the poet, cancelled the canon, and spat on literary aesthetics. He sees himself as the Plato and the Aristotle of literature, superior to the mere writer, a leader of an immortal band.

It is unforgiveable to quote onself, nevertheless I do so: twenty-four years ago I wrote in "Preliminaries" that " . . . fiction as knowledge is what we take away from the entire network of emotion, information and juxtaposition in fiction." By that I meant to indicate the intertwinings of human emotions and history itself, for no matter how apparently remote from the quotidian reality endlessly unfolded in the press and other outlets, the writer cannot escape his membership in his society and his calendar time; even by writing fantasy, his very choice of that mode can be seen as a political act. He may hate his own history, but he cannot separate himself from it this side of suicide.

In the exegesis, I attempted to distinguish between history and politics. Politics wedded to ideology, as it so often is, is foreign to the ideal of objective history, thus the term "political novel" is that fiction in which, deductively, character and events illustrate or prove an hypothesis concerning a special situation. If I were re-writing *Fiction as Knowledge* now, I should want to expand on the subject beyond the cursory broaching of the subject that the lecture-form required. I should also want to expand upon the quotations from Dilthey in the chapter on Proust, particularly, " . . . our analysis of lived experience and of self-understanding has shown that in the world of the mind, the individual is an object of absolute value, and indeed is the only such object that exists. This interest occupies us, apart from that practical interest which forces us to concern ourselves with men (for a good part of our life), whether in honorable or evil, foolish or vulgar ways." Dilthey's analysis of the subjective versus the objective, as it relates to fiction beyond Proust, my immediate concern, deserves a chapter in itself. Again, if I were writing now, I should want to expand on the brief mention of Adam Müller's insistence upon man as determined by his past, with his logical but to the post-Hitlerian mind, flawed belief that man is hardly conceivable apart from the State.

The temptation to re-write must be resisted, if only because the analyses of the past may have their own value, however slight, as paragraphs or footnotes to their time. As all ancients learn, one can neither re-live nor re-write the past. As for the validity of my analyses, I am perhaps foolishly optimistic. Montherlant, Malraux, Hemingway, and the rest of the cast will outlive the pit into which each succeeding generation casts its parents' idols, just as they will outlive the Dark Age of deconstruction, I am convinced. If the gods are good, I too hope to outlive that Dark Age. It will not be long.

FICTION AS KNOWLEDGE

The Modern Post-Romantic Novel

Preliminaries

A civilization unravels like a worn-out garment when men lose faith in their ability to define the present in relation to the past, when the act of definition itself becomes suspect, and when rationality is scorned in favor of feeling, intuition, mysticism, and magic. That we are deep in such a period, and have been since approximately 1950, is obvious. What may not be obvious are the implications for the arts of willed and studied ignorance, and specifically for the literary art of prose fiction.

Some such generalization lay behind the impulse to write the following chapters, which were first delivered as lectures to a Christian Gauss Seminar in Criticism at Princeton University. Although the lectures have been rewritten, I have retained some of the liberties that the lecture format permits. I doubt that I was alone in having been first amused, then appalled at the antihistorical bias so prevalent in the United States and in Europe over the past twenty years. Language breaks down; the very concept of standards is regarded as élitist, camp, or both; ignorance of past achievement makes for false and inflated judgment of contemporary work.

As I planned a counterattack it struck me that what is often missing from accounts of modern writing is awareness of the continuity between Romanticism and the Modern. I therefore fixed upon the term "post-Romantic," as opposed to "neo-Romantic," as useful and indeed crucial to a proper understanding of our own time. The post-Romantics are those

who, consciously or unconsciously, were aware of Romanticism as the last coherent and encompassing movement we
know in literary history. By their intellectual awareness of
Romanticism (Broch), their use of Romantic themes (Musil,
Hemingway), their awareness of history (Malraux, Faulkner),
the quality of their attention to Nature (Proust), or even through
parody of Romanticism (Broch, Montherlant), such writers
attest to the vitality of continuity. By implication they may
indicate that the garment of our civilization must not be permitted to unravel.

At least since the Russian Revolution of 1917 and its
apparent vindication of the Hegelian-Marxian hypothesis
concerning inevitable historical evolution, the entire complex
of ideas that we call "history" has become suspect to a considerable body of literate men. History has become the province of certain sociologists, of Marxist theoreticians, whether
European, American, or Asian; of "Cliometricians," barbarous
word; or of ideological propagandists on the far Right. Professional historians, in the meantime, have lost their bearings
and have come to distrust their own discipline. Since Croce
and Collingwood, we have had no philosopher of history wor-
thy of the name; Phenomenology with its profoundly antihistorical bias has shoved history aside. Outrageous events in fre-
netic succession would seem to have removed our appetite
for rational historical appraisal.

In literary criticism of the same period, an increasingly
similar pattern may be discerned. Nominalism and function-
alism have combined to question and often to deny the very
possibility of literary history,[1] to the degree that historical
problems of interpretation, together with the uses of history
in literature, are more often than not ignored. For those born
during or since World War II, myth-chasing through the

undergrowth of anthropology takes the place of traditional historical enquiry. The resulting indifference to tradition has produced a distortion in our conception of ourselves as moderns. Criticism that chooses to slight or to ignore history, I believe, is naïve. To take historical bearings afresh, in this case from the genre of the novel, is a deliberate attempt to challenge the antihistorical school and thus to correct some of our distortions.

The novel notoriously defies definition. Critics can only list attributes and describe individual novels, but if their lists and descriptions have anything in common, it is the element of history. Narrative, no matter how dominant or tenuous in the most experimental work, exists in time; it sets up in us expectations, comparisons, anticipations, or disappointments; it elicits judgments that depend finally upon our sense of time and events in their sequence. We contrast past to present, private to public, one set of manners to another, or we link episodes, fictional or "real," to the creation of a historical continuum. That continuum of itself does not constitute history, but it contributes to the formation of what I consider to be fiction as knowledge. The historical Romantic movement of the eighteenth and nineteenth centuries made history available to the novel through its emphasis on national entities possessing a past both mythic and recorded, and second through its emphasis upon the uniqueness of the individual, human person.

My thesis throughout is that the post-Romantics, working out from impulses and practices of writers in the historical Romantic period, came to understand fiction as a form of knowledge in which history may and frequently does equal illusion. That special form of illusion was given substance and authority by the cyclical idea of history. That remarkable idea, which derives from Vico, is most widely known through

Nietzsche's evocation of *"die ewige Wiederkunft,"* [2] "the
eternal return." Although the idea of cyclical history has been
spurned as mystical by recent professional historians and has
been excoriated for producing work so spurious as Oswald
Spengler's *The Decline of the West,* it nevertheless proved
attractive to Romanticism, just as it offers a wide range of
possibilities to the novelist. The cyclical idea enhances the
illusion through which the novelist's kind of knowledge can
be conveyed. Such illusion is most obvious in Faulkner's
work, where a rapid reading of *Light in August* or *Absalom,
Absalom!* might tempt one to the conclusion that Faulkner
intends history to *be* illusion, and that illusion is the only
reality. "Illusion" in Faulkner's case, illusion as allied to
historical knowledge, however, has a special, precise meaning according to which the processes of fiction at work in
narrative constitute history.

Those processes and that history can hardly be para-
phrased; fiction as knowledge is what we take away from the
entire network of emotion, information, and juxtaposition in
fiction. It can clearly be seen in evidence, as I shall try to
demonstrate, in the disparity between the early volumes of
Proust's *À la recherche du temps perdu* and the final volume,
in which current public event closes in on the comparatively
esoteric matter of the preliminary volumes. Fiction as knowledge is directly, although subtly, apparent in Malraux's
novels; so much so that many readers failed to apprehend
Malraux's fiction as fiction, as knowledge through illusion,
and criticized him as though he were writing political history.
Maurice Blanchot sets the matter in order when he writes of
Malraux: "Agreed that he creates only his own universe, but
the movement of that interior universe coincides with the
movement of history, and thus he also creates history, which is
to say, the sense of history." [3] Fiction as knowledge in post-

Romantic practice clears away long-standing confusion in many minds between time in history and time as continuity. History as time, or continuity, having a beginning and an end is of course Christian and apocalyptic. The contribution of the post-Romantic novelist is to demonstrate that a sense of time is given through history; this is Proust's great insight, as in quite other contexts it is Faulkner's, Broch's, Musil's, and Malraux's. Historical Romanticism, then, provided a powerful source of energy, a source still in good working order, despite Georg Lukács, who would subtract history from Romanticism, a movement that he sees as trivial and reactionary. I shall try to restate the Romantic assumption that history can be retold according to the necessity of the teller.

The very term "Romanticism" at once involves us in a semantic wrangle. People of impeccable semantic manners often avoid the word altogether, or they slide over it with a shrug of despair. Since 1924, when A. O. Lovejoy published his article "On the Discrimination of Romanticisms," [4] critics have tended indiscriminately to discriminate Romanticism out of existence. The efforts of Jacques Barzun and René Wellek to answer Lovejoy were made ineffectual by their distance in time from the source of the attack. [5] The damage, perhaps irreparable, had long been done.

By now, therefore, a useful, necessary, and indeed inevitable conception has been virtually lost to criticism. [6] Yet one must agree with René Wellek that a perfectly identifiable historical movement labeled "Romanticism" did take place in Western Europe and in the United States from the late eighteenth to the mid-nineteenth century, and I would add that a version of historical Romanticism has not only survived but triumphed. The failure to identify Romanticism in the modern movement in art is therefore absurd, a symptom of a disorder in our culture — the willful ignoring of history — that could result in a grubby end to a splendid complex of mind and imagination that has persisted since the Renaissance.

A representative example of that disorder is provided in an anthology published in 1965, entitled *The Modern Tradition.*[7] The editors remark in their preface the difficulty of defining "modern"; they allude in passing and imprecisely to historical Romanticism, and they conclude by writing that they do not mean to define "modern" anyway, but only to give the reader documents with which to construct his own definition, rather like a cake mix. The editors' categories of the modern, nine of them, are Symbolism, Realism, Nature, Cultural History, the Unconscious, Myth, Self-Consciousness, Existence, and Faith. At least seven of the nine belong to the definition of Romanticism that I shall develop, which is simply to suggest that the modern movement in literary art is Romantic at base, not to be conceived without Romanticism. The writers included in the nine categories are as predictable as they are, in company, indigestible; that fact, in turn, emphasizes that the editors cannot (or will not) define "modern," because the modern movement is a movement or manifestation that is philosophically uneasy with itself. It is so, I believe, in large degree for lack of the conception of post-Romanticism.

The literary movement called "Romanticism" and conventionally dated from roughly 1790 to roughly 1850 is hard to define because, for one thing, the conventional chronology is faulty. The beginning is ill-dated because the Germans, creators of so much that was Romantic, were reluctant to give up their notions of Classicism. They were even more reluctant to abandon their teacher and master, Goethe (whom Montherlant refers to as Goeoeoeoethe) to "early" or "pre-" Romanticism. The end is ill-dated because literary historians and philosophers cannot agree on precisely what Romanticism is and where its limits lie. That confusion has been further confounded for us in English by the efforts of T. E. Hulme, Ezra Pound, and T. S. Eliot to devise a new ·Classicism and to deride the poetic practice of the traditional masters of Romanticism. In his essay "Shelley and Keats," for example, Eliot expressed his dislike for Keats's "egotism," and observes that Shelley maintains "shabby ideals" which become less than palatable because they are muddled up with intuition.[8] Shelley is fluent, but in his verse Eliot finds "a good deal which is just bad jingling."[9] Comment such as Eliot's and confusion about Romanticism may be explained by the notion that the post-Romantics literally are ourselves, for better or worse, in the uneasy modern world. It is always difficult, if not impossible, to define oneself to oneself, and equally difficult to accept a movement that performs the task for us, however lacking in finesse and finality that definition may be.

At the same time, dubious philosophical explanation together with inertia has substituted for the reality a definition of Romanticism that does conform to the traditional dates, 1790 to 1850. It is that definition which applies to the Germans, but not necessarily to the English or the French. It is the view that emphasizes the authenticity of emotion over rationality; the alleged incapacity of the Romantic artist to accept and to cope with the present, objective reality. It is the view that emphasizes historical quaintness, the cult of genius, the otherworldly and metaphysical as opposed to the things of this world, the physical. It emphasizes the grotesque, the grandiose, overstated, overheated, comic-strip notions of the artist as inspired madman, rakehell, Byronic doomed hero: flamboyant, extra-human, and more than a little ludicrous. Such a vision or its equivalent seems to have been in the minds of those American enemies of Romanticism, Irving Babbitt and Paul Elmer More; and even though a later generation may reject their inhumane humanism, it often agrees that Romanticism as a movement came to an end a good, comfortable time ago, and that where it may survive as a habit of mind, it is unfortunate but not important.

Another and possibly more accurate view is that of Romanticism, both the historical and the post-Romantic varieties, as a complex, often contradictory, remarkably enduring impulse in Western thought and aesthetics, the full outlines of which we are now only beginning to take in. In this view, Romanticism is predominantly intellectual and rational rather than anti-intellectual; one of its highest accomplishments was to devise, mainly through Fichte's and Schelling's assertion of the boundlessness of human reason, ways to use caprice and illogicality, ways to accommodate in art the impulses of intuition and imagination which the later Enlightenment had theorized out of existence. Historical Romanticism, in this view, did not oppose the Enlightenment. Rather it took from the Enlightenment its intellectualism, its didacticism, and its ethical bias The points of emphasis of Romanticism, however, were quite different from, but not antithetical to, those of the Enlightenment.

It was John Locke who made possible the subjectivity of Romantic literature, for "If truth is the joining or separating of signs, which represent ideas as impressions, then the study of truth is the study of experience within. This does not mean a flight from reality, but rather that the locus of reality must be found within rather than without." [10] Jacques Rivière summarized all this when he wrote that "It is only with the advent of Romanticism that the literary act came to be conceived as a sort of *raid on the absolute* and its result as a revelation." [11] Rivière's marvelous phrase, a "raid on the absolute," contains all the heady theorizing of Fichte in the *Wissenschaftslehre*, as well as Novalis' conviction, "The fairy tale is, as it were, the

canon of poetry—everything poetic must have a fairy-tale
quality about it. The poet adores chance." [12] Those aspects of
Romanticism which combined to organize Rivière's "raid" on
the absolute are readily familiar; the intention here is no more
than to sketch them in.

A far more controversial view of Romanticism than any of
the preceding is that of Jacques Barzun. He contends that
Romanticism and Realism are not two conflicting movements
in the arts, but that Realism as well as Naturalism are simply
manifestations of Romanticism. Proof, for Barzun, lies in a
proper historical understanding of the roots, practices, and
impulses of Romanticism. According to his reading, it is
Classicism that is abstract, imprecise, and woolly, and Romanticism that is precise, concerned with exact observation and
with the proliferation of detail.[13] Barzun classifies Romanticism
from 1790 to 1850 as "unspecialized," a time of enormous productivity in all the arts. The next three phases after 1850 show
efforts at "specialization, selection, refinement and intensi-
fication." The years 1850 to 1885 are the years of Realism;
from 1875 to 1905 the years of Symbolism; and the years after
1850 produce Naturalism, which in literature continues at
least until World War II.[14] Whether or not one agrees with
Barzun, and I do, his argument concerning the breadth and
continuity of Romanticism is in welcome contrast to the conception of Romanticism as a movement as dead and gone as
the medieval rhymed chronicle, or sixteenth-century Euphu-
ism.

CHAPTER 1

Romanticism and Modern Fiction: Proust

If we want to test the truth of proposals about the continuing validity of basic Romantic impulses, it is imperative to examine the early Romantics' sense of history, their apprehension of the past, and some of the ways in which that apprehension proved useful to writers, as well as to later historians. Standard accounts of the genesis of Romanticism, particularly those in English, fail to emphasize the importance of historical theory for the first Romantics. Such accounts appear to agree with Nietzsche, a hostile witness, when he wrote: "A Romantic is an artist whose great self-distrust is a source of creative energy—one who looks away from himself and his surroundings, and thus looks backwards." [1] Herder in particular has not been given his just due. It is not too much to say that Herder was as significant for the nineteenth century as Freud has been for the twentieth. Despite long-windedness and occasional lugubriousness, Herder's *Ideen zur Philosophie der Geschichte der Menschheit* (1784–1791) embodied a philosophy of history that was electrifying in its implications. The famous first sentence of the *Ideen*, "Vom Himmel muss unsere

Philosophie der Geschichte des menschlichen Geschlechts anfangen," suggests his tone, but it does not suggest the revolutionary implications of the matter to follow: Herder's intuition of the unity of human history, of the value of the past for the present, and his simultaneous insistence that within the unity of humanity lies diversity, a diversity to be studied in language and customs and to be seen to constitute nations. In other terms, implicit in Herder's work was the entire area that we call social anthropology, together with the elements of a theory of individuality and of national identity.

In passing, one notes that more than forty years before Herder's *Ideen,* Giambattista Vico had anticipated many of Herder's conclusions and that Herder knew Vico's work.[2] What is pertinent, however, is that Herder was read fairly widely, whereas Vico was read not at all in his lifetime (his masterpiece, *Scienza nuova,* was not published in final form until after his death in January, 1744). Romanticism, in short, was ready for Herder, but the Enlightenment had not been ready for Vico.

Before Herder and before Romanticism, no one had attempted a proper philosophy of history. Exemplary events and exemplary characters were singled out in early histories for their exemplary qualities; they were the classicists' classics, frozen in time, or rather frozen out of time, timeless. Although Jean-Jacques Rousseau was hardly a philosopher of history, and although he did not think historically, he contributed to the new conception by his "sympathy"—the word is Collingwood's—for the past, by his evocation of human quality in history through his speculations on the nature of primitive, pastoral society. The upshot of all this for Romanticism was, first, awareness of history, and second, awareness of the self, the human self in history as well as apart from history.

The early Romantic awareness of history may be seen in the work of the gifted Friedrich von Hardenberg, Novalis (1772–1801). He was a civil servant and a close student of the natural sciences, but we know him primarily as an imaginative writer and visionary. Despite his visionary quality, Novalis' conception of history denies the cliché of Romantic escape, of Romantic abstraction, and of Romantic irresponsibility. On the one hand, Novalis regarded the thirteenth century as the Golden Age; we must notice his terms of reference in the first sentence of *Die Christenheit oder Europa:* "Those were fine, splendid days, when Europe was a Christian land, a single Christian unity; one great common interest united the most far-flung provinces of this vast, spiritual kingdom." [3] Novalis' intellectual nostalgia might appear to be an example of the vision of history as escape into an idealized past, a false and deluded projection, willed, and in the pejorative sense of the word, rhetorical, but his historical thought here, as elsewhere, is controlled by his historical principle, "Die Gegenwart ist das Differential der Funktion der Zukunft und Vergangenheit," [4] which might best be translated by Unamuno's frequently repeated, "The present is nothing more than the past trying to become the future."

Along with Novalis' conception of an ideal past, which may also be seen in his unfinished novel, *Heinrich von Ofterdingen,* went a great many reflections about the nature of the State: many the product of Novalis' coming to terms with the French Revolution and its aftermath, some prophetic, some naïve, some alarming to our hindsight, but all based in the new — shall we say modern? — post-Herder mode of political thought. The following political observations, called "fragments" and obviously modeled on the aphorisms of the Enlightenment, are from *Glauben und Liebe* (1798), and from *Fragmente und Studien* (1797–1798; 1799–1800): "Every

citizen is a civil servant." [5] "One great fault of our states is
that one sees the State too infrequently. The State should be
everywhere visible, and every man should be characterized
as a citizen. Could one not introduce marks of distinction and
uniforms everywhere? Anyone who regards this as insigni-
ficant disregards an essential part of our nature." [6] "We *know*
too little about the State. There should be heralds of the State,
preachers of patriotism. As it is, most citizens are on a rather
indifferent, almost hostile footing with the State." [7] And from
the *Allgemeinen Brouillon* (1798–1799), "The perfect citizen
lives entirely in the State; he has no property outside the
State." [8]

If such statements look odd to the modern eye, it is well
to recall that Novalis was brought up in the Moravian Pietist
tradition, one that led him to equate the family with the State.
The German term for Moravian, *Herrnhuter*, means literally
"the Lord my shepherd"; for Novalis, the ideal shepherd was
Joseph II of Austria, that ill-starred reformer who tried by
fiat, well before their time, to introduce many of the reforms
associated with the benefits of the French Revolution. The
Pietist tradition further meant the rejection of Rousseau's
idea of natural right, of the State as the embodiment of a con-
tract between government and governed. Novalis looked
forward, not to the Hitlerian Fascist State, but to a "State of
States," a universal republic in true freedom under religious
guidance.[9] Novalis was a spiritual progenitor, not of Ezra
Pound who ranted on wartime radio for Mussolini, but of the
T. S. Eliot who wrote *The Idea of a Christian Society*. It is
further corrective to recall that Novalis was not a nationalist.
He was both utopian, like many Romantics, and playful, rare
in German letters. With considerable humor he wrote, "The
European is as superior to the German as the German is to the
Saxon, and the Saxon to the inhabitant of Leipzig." [10] Novalis'

historical consciousness was most fully enunciated when he wrote this Faulknerian statement: "We bear the burdens of our fathers, just as we have inherited their goods, and we actually live in the past and the future and are nowhere less at home than in the present." [11] Such words move close to the essence of the relationship between early Romanticism and the post-Romantic novel, for they evoke a theme that novelists have come to repeatedly: the impact, tragic in implication, of a virtually palpable past upon an impalpable present. If Novalis' words are Faulkernian, they are also Proustian, as I shall try to demonstrate presently.

Novalis' view of the State, his idea of the nation, is close to that of Adam Müller, "the political philosopher of Romanticism," in Hans Kohn's words. Müller believed that the State was established for man, but that man was indissolubly part of the State, and *determined by its past.* "Man," Müller wrote, "cannot be imagined outside of the state . . . the state . . . is the totality of all human concern." [12] In spite of a religious cast, Müller's political philosophy registers dramatically the separation of history from theology, from prophecy, from revelation, and from those complexes of thought and association which in the past had prevented the Chronicle or the Voltairean polemic from being what we, with slight arrogance, call "true" history. Until such separation occurred, history could not serve the arts as it was to do from the beginning of the nineteenth century on. At the same time, it is necessary to one's understanding of much nineteenth-century literature to notice that implicit in Müller's insistence that man is *determined* by the past lies a powerful source of energy for the historical and the post-Romantic periods.

On the one side is the temptation to determinism and its axiom that man's freedom is cruelly limited by his nature, his surroundings, and by his very genes, the view that leads to

literary Naturalism. On the other side is a powerful impulse
to a philosophy of freedom, one best summarized in Henri
Bergson's *Essai sur les données immédiates de la conscience*
(1889), and one best characterized as Romantic at base, for in
that essay as in much of his later work, Bergson, wittingly or
not, evokes a strain in Romantic thought that derives from men
so disparate as Fichte and Byron, Schelling and Emily
Brontë. In the *Essai*, Bergson conceives of consciousness as
the opposite of the external world of objective, individual,
measurable things. Consciousness is indivisible, dependent
upon the succession of mental states, a temporal process, but
not merely upon succession and temporality. Bergson opposes
traditional empiricism in asserting that mental states inter-
penetrate one another; past and present lose simple continuity
in time as the free consciousness edits and frames experience.
The process is like that in which we apprehend a film. The
film is made up of thousands of frames which run in succession before our eyes, yet our final conception of that film is
not the product of the succession of frames as succession. The
frames exist in time, they have sequence, but our conception
or interpretation of the film as a whole melds past and present;
our conception is not determined by sequence. In experience
at large, the present contains the past, but it is not determined
by it. Man is free in the vital activity by which in effect he
creates the past by his own mental activity. He is not passive,
not determined by the succession of the "frames" of the past.
The present is a creative present, not a process of supine
resignation to the inevitable.

Something of Bergson's conception of freedom is present
in Novalis' musings about history and about the Romantic
revolution that he helped to lead. By theory and example, he
demonstrates the careful movement of a writer's mind over
public ground, together with his apprehension, in the vast

wake of the French Revolution, that such ground was, in fact, public.

Before moving to imaginative literature, however, one must consider the force of argument of that magnificent monster of the nineteenth century, Georg Wilhelm Friedrich Hegel. Although Herder was fairly well known, it was Hegel who dominated nineteenth-century thought, and Hegel who in one sense denied an important aspect of Herder's insight. I refer to Herder's principle of the unity of man and nature, that principle which was was so fundamental in historical Romantic theory and practice. In his lectures on the Philosophy of History delivered in 1822 and 1823, Hegel developed his principle of *Geist* (mind, or spirit) as opposed to nature. "At the outset we must observe," Hegel said, "that world history takes precedence in the area of *Geist*. 'World' contains in itself both psychic and physical nature; physical nature simultaneously is contained in world history, and we may not ignore this fundamental fact. But the essential is *Geist* and the course of its development. We do not need to take nature into account here, for nature in itself constitutes a system of knowledge [literally *Vernunft*, reason], the elements of which are merely relative to *Geist*." [13] For Hegel, world spirit dominates history in a progression marked by a liberation from nature; as long as spirit is subject to nature, progress is impossible. Nature, then, has only negative significance; it is no more than background, terrain, upon which the history of the world comes to pass. Hegel shared with Herder, however, the hypothesis that terrain, climate, and locale establish the character of specific peoples of the world.

Whether we are to regard Nature as mere setting, an amphitheater for the play of phenomena, or whether Nature is a link to the infinite, a necessary quality of man's spiritual life, was the question at issue between the party of Hegel, on

the one side, and the party of Herder, on the other. That opposition was to remain a fiery and, for art, a productive issue
throughout the nineteenth century (in the United States, well
into the twentieth).

In at least two other respects, Hegel's philosophy of history was tremendously important to Romantic art: first, in his
emphasis upon time; and second, in his notion of the heroic
in history. For Hegel, time is the "now." The now "has an
'enormous right'" — good Hegelian phrase — "because only
the present truly 'is,' in contrast to what is already past and
what does not yet exist. The individual, finite now is nevertheless only a point in time which 'stands opposed' to the infinite
whole of time, which is an eternal circle." [14] The movement of
time is a dialectic in which the future becomes the past, while
the evanescent present moves inevitably into the future. The
true present is the eternity which is immanent in time. The
present alone *is;* it is to be sure the outcome of the past, but it
bears the future within it. In Hegel's logic, the present is
thus eternity. In his Preface to the *Philosophie des Rechts,*
Hegel wrote: "An arrangement according to class in philosophy is definitely not imposed from outside, in accordance
with one or several arbitrary systems already to hand. It is
rather the recognition of differences immanent in the concepts themselves." [15] That is, he would distinguish in the out-
ward form, that which is immanent and eternal.

Hegel's definition of time applies as well to his occasionally mysterious concept of *Geist.* The spirit of world history
is simply there; it is present, the given. It is not already past,
nor is it yet to come; it is completely now. Hegel wrote that
"Insofar as we consider only the idea of spirit, and all stages
of world history may be regarded only as the appearance of
spirit, we have then found that however grand the stages of
the past, it is only the present that we engage, for philosophy,

insofar as it is concerned with truth, must ever concern itself with the present. Nothing that has occurred in the past is lost to the present, for the idea is of the present, of the undying spirit. That is, it is not past nor is it not in the process of becoming, but it substantially is in being. One repeats that the present frame contains within it all stages of the past." [16] Through the fog of language we may see that Hegel is affirming the principle of cyclic recurrence in history, a principle of dubious merit as history, but rich in implication for literature.

Hegel's idea of the heroic is restricted by the fact that it is difficult for us to find in his writing the recognizably human, even though it is intermittently there. *Geist* almost sweeps away *Mensch*. Hegel's notorious historicism produced along the way a rather vulgar notion of success as the token of individuality in history. That is, only those men are valuable who are products of the high plane upon which world history moves; the successful individual is he who combines in his person "national spirit" and the "idea" that he was destined to embody and to dominate.[17] Bonaparte beyond all others was that historical individual, both for Hegel and for Goethe. And, we might add, for Stendhal, whose work is often a fascinating projection, or reduction, of Hegelian philosophy.

One singles out Hegel's theory of time and his theory of greatness for their relevance to much Romantic literature of the historical period, but also for their value as links to the post-Romantic. Theories of time at once remind us of the degree to which Romantic literature was epistemological: a literature of discovery, *Bildung*, and a literature about discovery, about perceptions of the self and of the exterior world. That epistemological element survives, even though it has undergone a sea change, in Joyce, in Unamuno, in Baroja, in Broch, Musil, and Mann; above all in Proust. And the role of the great man as developed in Goethe, Hegel, Victor Cousin, and Carlyle produced not only the over familiar figure of the Romantic hero: Hugo's Jean Valjean, Melville's Pierre, or Emily Brontë's Heathcliff; it produced that intermediate, ironic hero of Stendhal, Julien Sorel, Count Mosca; Flaubert's Frédéric Moreau; and it also produced the modern anti-hero: Leopold Bloom, Lucky Jim, unlucky Herzog.

Yet it is at once clear that neither the Romantic conception of history as we see it in Novalis' work, nor Hegelian dialectic, nor even Romantic irony in the manner of E. T. A. Hoffmann, is capable of accounting for the range and complexity of the post-Romantic writers under discussion in this book. To measure the distance separating Stendhal's Count Mosca from Musil's Ulrich, the man without qualities, to take just one example, it is rewarding to look to Wilhelm Dilthey (1833–1911). In Dilthey's writings, which embraced both history and aesthetics, we come close to familiar, modern ground, yet we remain in essentially Romantic territory. Dilthey's posthumously published essay, "Das Verstehen anderer Personen und ihrer Lebensäusserungen" ("The Understanding of Other Persons and Their Life-Expressions") is of first importance, I think, to our comprehension of the recent past.

Three quotations are to the point. Dilthey's explanation of how a work comes into being is quintessentially Romantic; at first glance it looks like the work of Coleridge. Dilthey wrote that "Because of the conditions determining its creation, . . . no truly great work of art can reflect elements foreign to its creator: indeed its existence is completely independent of his." [18] Although this may evoke Chapter XIV of *Biographia Literaria*, Dilthey's emphasis on the absolute independence of the work of art goes beyond Coleridge and the familiar vegetable metaphor of the Romantics, to approach the conception of the phenomenologists.

The second quotation has to do with Dilthey's theory of objective mind: "By objective mind, I understand the manifold forms in which features common to individuals are objectified in the world of the senses. In the objective mind the past is always present to us. Its domain reaches from ways of life and forms of social intercourse to the complex of aims developed by society, to customs, rights, the State, religion, art, science and philosophy. Even works of genius represent a common store of ideas, inner life, and ideals in a particular age and environment." [19] Here Dilthey adopts a familiar Hegelian idea, but he departs from Hegel in his humane extension of *Geist* away from the windy abstractions of history to the immediate and the everyday lives of ordinary men.

That process of adaptation is even clearer in a third quotation from Dilthey: "Understanding always has something individual as its object, and in its higher forms it argues from the inductive complex given in a work or a life, to the life-complex of a person or a work. But our analysis of lived experience and of self-understanding has shown that in the world of the mind, the individual is an object of absolute value, and indeed is the only such object that exists. As such we concern ourselves with him, not only as an instance of general human nature, but as an individual whole. This interest occupies us, apart from that practical interest which forces us to concern ourselves with men (for a good part of our life), whether in honorable or evil, foolish or vulgar, ways. The secret of the individual draws us, for its own sake, into ever new and more profound attempts to understand it, and it is in such understanding that the individual and mankind in general and its creations are revealed to us. . . . The objective mind and the power of the individual to interpret it together determine the world of mind. History rests on the understanding of these two." [20]

Here Dilthey is defining his conception of history, but his definition is also rich in implication for art, for the art of prose fiction in particular. The establishment of the individual "as an object of value" had been a central achievement of the Romantics. Dilthey perceived the necessity, after Kant and Hegel (and despite Nietzsche), to bring the individual *into* history. In Dilthey's scheme, the individual does not transcend history in a metaphysical leap, nor exist only in the awkward garments of greatness. Neither is the individual transcended *by* history. "History," again in Dilthey's phrase, "rests on the understanding of these two": the individual, and mankind in general. By implication, Dilthey also frees art from the constrictions of Darwinian determinism, just as his subtle conception of individualism may aid us to grasp the importance of what might be called the imaginative epistemology of post-Romantic novelists.

Imaginative epistemology is fully apparent in Marcel Proust's *À la recherche du temps perdu*, the dominant and all-encompassing burden of which is perception itself: how the narrator sees himself and his world, and how his perceptions, varying in time, conspire to give him an acceptable and consistent view of that world in both psychological and historical terms. Proust's work defies and resists conventional analysis, which defiance and resistance are a measure of its greatness. Here I want no more than to juxtapose *Du côté de chez Swann*, Proust's beginning, with *Le Temps retrouvé*, his ending, in order to place in focus (admittedly in inexact focus because of narrative compression) those aspects of the whole which best serve my continuing discussion.

Proust's novel, together with the novels discussed in subsequent chapters, is first of all post-Romantic. By that I mean not simply that it follows upon Romanticism in point of time, but that his work is occasioned and made feasible by Romanticism. We hear first and throughout that central voice of the narrator.[21] Despite the orchestration of the novel, the wonderfully complex manner in which the narrator's life folds and unfolds upon us, Proust's consciousness of self, his relentless insistence upon the centrality of that self, is a product of the Romantic discovery of self and of the Romantic insistence upon the primacy of individuality, of the ego, the *je*, the "I." A related and perhaps equally obvious fact is that the narrator's entire experience, quite apart from and in addition to the magical manner of the narration, constitutes a traditional Romantic form, that of the *Bildungsroman* (the novel of education or formation). As in the case of Goethe's *Wilhelm Meister* or Stendhal's *Le Rouge et le noir,* the form of the *Bildungsroman* offered a picaresque looseness of outline, together with the opportunity to exploit one's Romantic fascination with the problem of moral progress, or regress, through the world and through society. Although Proust's conception of time, together with his complex narrative techniques, may disguise the element of *Bildung,* it is undeniably present and basic.

À *la recherche du temps perdu* is related to Romanticism in still another quality: in Proust's apprehension of physical nature, in the narrator's almost mystical merging of himself in the physical setting, in the conveyed conviction of an entire area of fineness of sensibility and the possibility of moral purity deriving from nature. Nature as Proust's narrator senses it is not the marmoreal nature of the French Romantic tradition, that of Lamartine or Hugo; it is rather idyllic. The season is almost always spring or lush summer. Combray as it emerges through the narrator's memory is more than a village in the Île-de-France: it is an Eden, a gorgeous place altogether with its trees, its *aubépines,* the famous hawthorn, the roses at Tansonville, the Vivonne River, the boys fishing. It is not a

theological Eden as depicted by Milton in *Paradise Lost*, but
Eden as painted by Renoir, with one eye on nature and the
other on Botticelli's *Primavera*. Not surprisingly, Proust's
idyll, his Eden, is associated with the narrator as a boy, with
a boy's innocence and freshness of perception. The evocation
is always that of a world lost through knowledge, of nature
become unnatural through the narrator's illness, which is
both immediate cause and symbol of his loss of the natural,
mainly botanical world. It is literally unnatural through the
boy's, and later the man's, exposure to various kinds of sexual
inversion. That process of loss of the natural world is at once
archetypical, mythical by implication, and intensely Romantic.

Romanticism made nature available to art through the
identification of the natural with the Good, and through the
Romantic conviction that the supremacy of art over all other
human activity is the result of the artist's fundamental, organic
relationship to nature. Proust's evocations of nature through
landscape above all are visual, but we know that he was
impatient with the mere description of objects in the manner
of the realists and naturalists, his contemporaries.[22] At the
same time, he did not, like Lamartine, perceive natural objects
as emblems or symbols. Proust was far closer to Wordsworth
(and possibly to Hardy) in the quality of his attention to nature
than he was to any writer in the French tradition. The whole of
À la recherche du temps perdu resembles *The Prelude* in
theme, in content, and with due allowance for difference in
genre, in technique. The place of memory in both works,
whether voluntary or involuntary, "mémoire" or "souvenir,"
is virtually identical. Proust enunciates the terms and his
theory of them, but Wordsworth apprehends and uses in his
poetry precisely parallel modes.

In *The Prelude*, for example, Wordsworth's account of

his years at Cambridge (Book Sixth) attaches to objects; objects lead to reverie upon the dimensions of meaning, and finally to belief in Wordsworth's version of a "Supreme Existence," Thus the "lofty elms" and . . . /A single tree

> With sinuous trunk, boughs exquisitely wreathed,
> Grew there; an ash which Winter for himself
> Decked out with pride, and with outlandish grace:
> Up from the ground, and almost to the top,
> The trunk and every master branch were green
> With clustering ivy, and the lightsome twigs
> And outer spray profusely tipped with seeds
> That hung in yellow tassels, while the air
> Stirred them, not voiceless. Often have I stood
> Foot-bound uplooking at this lovely tree
> Beneath a frosty moon.   (ll. 76–87, 1850 edition.)

Compare Wordsworth's ivy on the ash tree with Proust's narrator's reflections upon how the walks on the Méséglise Way and the Guermantes Way revealed natural objects which in turn contributed to his intellectual development:

The flowers which played then among the grass, the water which rippled past in the sunshine, the whole landscape which served as environment to their apparition lingers around the memory of them still with its unconscious or unheeding air; and, certainly, when they were slowly scrutinised by this humble passer-by, by this dreaming child—as the face of a king is scrutinised by a petitioner lost in the crowd—that scrap of nature, that corner of a garden could never suppose that it would be thanks to him that they would be elected to survive in all their most ephemeral details; and yet the scent of hawthorn which strays plundering along the hedge from which, in a little while, the dog-roses will have banished it, a sound of footsteps followed by no echo, upon a gravel path, a bubble formed at the side of a waterplant by the current, and formed only to burst—my exaltation of mind has borne them with it, and has succeeded in making them traverse all these successive years, while all around them the once-trodden ways have vanished, while those who thronged those ways, and even the memory of those who thronged those trodden ways, are dead.[23]

Shortly after this meditation, the narrator reflects: "It is because I *believed in things*, in people, while I was wandering among them, that the things, the people that they taught me to know, these alone I still take seriously and still give me joy." [24]

Between the narrator's apprehension of physical nature and his hard-headed insistence upon things, on the one hand, and the absence in his makeup of the final Romantic leap into the transcendental, on the other hand, lies Proust's post-Romanticism. Nature does not reveal a Supreme Existence to the narrator, as it does to Wordsworth; nature reveals rather *"joie,"* a function of the self that is in large part Romantic. We may say, then, that the distance from the Supreme Existence to Proustian *"joie"* is the distance from the historically Romantic to the post-Romantic.

Proust's link between his post-Romantic conception of the self and history is, logically and in fact, time. Although one need not disagree with the critic who tells us that not time but spatial form is what Proust creates in his presentation of time past and time present,[25] it is also true within another range of meaning that time is undeniably of the essence in the novel. It is central to the title of the whole, *À la recherche du temps perdu*, and to the final volume, *Le Temps retrouvé*, a fact that may be overlooked in the English titles of Scott Moncrieff (*Remembrance of Things Past*) and Frederick A. Blossom (*The Past Recaptured*), but is underlined in the 1970 translation by Andreas Mayor of the final volume (*Time Regained*). That famous discovery related in *Le Temps retrouvé* by which the narrator perceives that his mission is to write a book, to cover the very time, or let us say history, that we have experienced in the preceding volumes, is not only a triumph of perception; it is at the same time the discovery of history, a discovery made possible through history as well as through the theory of the writer's art that the narrator simultaneously develops. That rounding off of the novel, that turning back of the narrative upon itself, may suggest Vico's *ricorsi* or Hegel's cyclical hypothesis of historical movement.[26] Hegel's sense of the "now," of the true present as the eternity immanent in time, is so close to Proust's narrator's sense of time as to suggest direct borrowing.

Proust's "totems," in Samuel Beckett's useful term, the madeleine, the church steeples, the uneven paving in the Guermantes' forecourt, the starched napkin, all these are not only the signals or stimuli by which the narrator relives his own past; he relives his own history, and he moves in the final volume from his own individual, private history to exterior history, and to those incidents and changes in society at large that make up what we call political history. Earlier on, from the first volume through *La Fugitive*, the sixth, politics come through to us peripherally: in the figure of M. de Norpois, an object of satire, or through references to the Dreyfus case, which are presented mainly in terms of manners. The Dreyfus case has slight historical validity compared to its value for Proust in establishing a wide range of social attitudes. The overwhelming mass of material of the first six volumes, in short, is concerned with the personal: with the narrator's decline into illness, his affair with Albertine, his jealousy, his awareness of society, and with the social cast that embodies the sub-themes of the novel. In *Le Temps retrouvé*, to the contrary, Proust suddenly plunges us into history.

At the beginning of the volume, incidents or characters that earlier belonged to the narrator's personal intuitions change. In the course of a few pages, historical persons are alluded to in abundance: Robert Louis Stevenson, the Goncourts, Flaubert, Sainte-Beuve, Balzac, Charpentier, Romain

Rolland, Nietzsche, and Renoir. Now Proust sets time and place exactly. We are at Tansonville, then Paris; the year is 1916. The atmosphere of the city is like that of 1793.[27] The wartime atmosphere of Paris is sharply, satirically to be sure, and accurately evoked. The Dreyfusards have become respectable; the system of military draft is described. Mme Verdurin, of all people, is on the telephone daily to military GHQ; society seeks her out for the accuracy of her rumours about the course of the war. "In conversation, when she was announcing the news, Mme Verdurin would say 'we' when she meant France" (p. 43).

Seeing aircraft on patrol near Paris, the narrator assures himself that the planes do not remind him of Albertine or of the planes they had seen in their last afternoon together at Versailles; the entire passage is full of evocations of Albertine, we well know.[28] That is, Proust continues to weave fictional matter into the historical matter that tends to displace it. Bloch and Saint-Loup converse about war service, about fear of death in combat, and about reenlistment. Bloch announces the Kaiser's death: he has it on the best authority.[29] Gilberte writes about events at Tansonville, and in parenthesis the narrator remarks, ("This was in about September, 1914").[30] This and a second letter of two years later describe how the narrator's past literally has been blown out of existence:

Probably, like me, you did not imagine that obscure Roussainville and boring Méséglise, where our letters used to be brought from and where the doctor was once fetched when you were ill, would ever be famous places. Well, my dear friend, they have become forever a part of history, with the same claim to glory as Austerlitz or Valmy. The battle of Méséglise lasted for more than eight months; the Germans lost in it more than six hundred thousand men, they destroyed Méséglise, but they did not capture it. As for the short cut up the hill which you were so fond of and which we used to call the hawthorn path, where you claim that as a small child you fell in love with me (whereas I assure you in all truthfulness it was I who was in love with you), I cannot tell you how important it has become. The huge field of corn upon which it emerges is the famous Hill 307, which you must have seen mentioned again and again in the bulletins. The French blew up the little bridge over the Vivonne which you said did not remind you of your childhood as much as you would have wished, and the Germans have thrown other bridges over the river. For a year and a half they held one half of Combray and the French the other. [Pp. 77–78.]

Multitudes of commentators have remarked that Proust evoked his two "ways," Swann's Way and the Guermantes' Way, in order to give his work social texture and to provide sufficient reach for the narrator's casts of memory; further, that the two ways are merged through the deterioration of manners and of traditional, aristocratic efforts to keep society inviolable. One must emphasize all the more that in his final volume Proust literally blows up in warfare the two "ways" of Swann and the Guermantes. That violent destruction serves multiple purposes. It carries within it and is the exterior emblem of the burden of tragedy that pervades the novel. It makes historical social matter, which, up to that point, was first symbolic and second specific, mainly through Proust's talent for satire. The battle of Méséglise doubles us back once again to Combray, to the idyllic place, only to wipe it out, once and forever. History, that is to say, is the means by which Proust brings into final, terrifying, and tragic perspective the characters and events of the entire work.

It is history that precedes and renders poignant Proust's resolution of the work, the resolution of the dying narrator's total experience of life into the art of the novel that he must write. Proust's vision of history is contained in one of the loveliest passages in *Le Temps retrouvé*. The narrator is contrasting wartime Paris under the blackout with empty country scenes out of the remembered past at Combray, and with impressions of high seas at Balbec.

There were effects of moonlight normally unknown in towns, sometimes in the middle of winter even, when the rays of the moon lay outpoured upon the snow on Boulevard Haussmann, untouched now by the broom of any sweeper, as they would have lain upon a glacier in the Alps. Against this snow of bluish gold the silhouettes of the trees were outlined clear and pure, with the delicacy that they have in certain Japanese paintings or in certain backgrounds of Raphael; and on the ground at the foot of the tree itself there was stretched out its shadow as often one sees trees' shadows in the country at sunset, when the light inundates and polishes to the smoothness of a mirror some meadow in which they are planted at regular intervals. But by a refinement of exquisite delicacy the meadow upon which were displayed these shadows of trees, light as souls, was a meadow of paradise, not green but of a whiteness so dazzling because of the moonlight shining upon the jade-like snow that it might have been a meadow woven entirely from petals of flowering pear-trees. And in the squares the divinities of the public fountains, holding a jet of ice in their hand, looked like statues wrought in two different materials by a sculptor who had decided to marry pure bronze to pure crystal. On these exceptional days all the houses were black. But in the Spring, on the contrary, here and there, defying the regulations of the police, a private house, or simply one floor of a house, or even simply one room of one floor, had failed to close its shutters and appeared, mysteriously supported by dark impalpable shadows, to be no more than a projection of light, an apparition without substance. And the woman whom, if one raised one's eyes high above the street, one could distinguish in this golden penumbra, assumed, in this night in which one was oneself lost and in which she too seemed to be hidden away, the mysterious and veiled charm of an oriental vision. Then one passed on and nothing more interrupted the rustic tramp, tramp, wholesome and monotonous, of one's feet through the darkness. [Pp. 52–53.]

History makes inevitable the setting, for Proust cannot ignore the fact of the war. His meaning resides, as always, in images at once visual and intellectual, images which here are apprehensions of estrangement, of inhuman, untouched beauty, of enchanted unreality. Proust's vision of history also contains in advance the horrible scenes to follow of Charlus dodging about in the blackout on his way to the male brothel. The purposeful unreality of the Parisian landscape contains, too, Proust's insistence upon the place of art before history, his ultimate conviction that art can contain and therefore defeat history.

Proust's intense consciousness of time not only opens the book of history before him, but gives his work the impact of tragedy.[31] À la recherche du temps perdu is one of the few novels to which we may, without discomfort, apply the term "tragic." It is tragic in the dimensions of the narrator's unfolding awareness of himself, his social circumstances, and finally his historical circumstances, and also in his heroic resolution, however impossible of fulfillment, to defeat time and history through the art of fiction. Just as tragedy cannot exist without morality (an assertion one cannot here defend), so Proust's work, I believe, is moral. Its morality lies first in Proust's concern for manners, his exploration of conduct beyond manners, notably of homosexuality; in his views of art and artists; and in his narrator's positive "joie" at choosing unquestionably the life of art over the imminent physical death of the Guermantes set at the conclusion. His choice of life makes heroic his consciousness of his own mortality, and as in classical tragedy, we come away from Proust's novel in a state of simultaneous despair and exhilaration.

By emphasizing Romantic conceptions of history, I do not mean to imply that the Romantic view has endured. At least since Tolstoy, Romantic historicism in the manner of Hegel or Cousin has been punctured beyond repair. The example of Proust may suggest something else, that we in the

West are, in Marc Bloch's words, "extremely attentive" to the past of our civilization; that Romanticism extended the historian's range, and that history since the Romantics is a method of relocating the lost self, of seeking and uncovering identity. Not mere psychological identity, but the exterior contexts, social, political, and personal, that go to make up the human self in all its complexity. In such terms, the post-Romantic novelist obviously has a great deal to say to us. Proust's work provides us just one luminous example.

CHAPTER 2

Hermann Broch

If the argument is tenable that *À la recherche du temps perdu* bears an immediate and inevitable relationship to history, and that Proust's vision of history informs not only the exterior, social matter of the novel but also the interior, individual, and personal matter, then it becomes urgent that we know exactly what we intend by the central and apparently obvious term "history" in relation to prose fiction.

By "history" I do not mean politics, nor that variety of fiction in which events more or less imagined serve to illuminate power relationships in society, as in John Dos Passos' trilogy, *USA*, or Arthur Koestler's *Darkness at Noon*. In such novels history is present, but it is insisted upon and used deductively to prove some manner of ideological theorem. Invention and imagination are sacrificed to ideology, and what remains is often less fiction than tract.

By "history" I do not mean the historical novel, either. It is not now necessary to dispose of the popular version of the historical novel, that escapist narrative salted with sex, derring-do, and anachronism, unworthy offspring of Sir Walter Scott. The figure of Scott, however, must suggest his twentieth-

century Marxist champion, Georg Lukács. Lukács' influence
upon the post-World War II neo-Marxist or proto-Marxist
variety of criticism has been so pervasive that it is necessary
to say unmistakably why one does not agree with Lukács'
ideas about the historical novel and about the relationship between history and fiction. His argument in *Der historische
Roman* (1937)[1] is based on his explanation of Hegel's theory
of history, and simultaneously on a curiously sentimental version of that Marxist abstraction, "the people." Hegel, according to Lukács, improved upon the Enlightenment notion of
man's unalterable nature by seeing "a process in history, a
process propelled, on the one hand, by the inner motive forces
of history and which, on the other, extends its influence to all
the phenomena of human life, including thought. He sees the
total of life of humanity as a great historical process."[2] This
can mean anything one wants it to mean. For Lukács, it leads
to a theory of art as exclusively realistic, and to a theory that
the novel does not really exist until the entry of "the people"
into the process of history. The historical novel, indeed, constitutes the entire genre; any other approach amounts to an
empty and culpable aestheticism. The people enter history
through "social transformation," which is to say, through
revolution. The novel begins with Scott, whose mind was
formed by the revolution of 1688, and takes its modern and
enduring form after 1789. Lukács writes of the French Revolutionary wars, "Thus in this mass experience of history the
national element is linked on the one hand with problems of
social transformation; and on the other, more and more people
become aware of the connection between national and world
history."[3]

Despite the Hegelian echoes in the above quotation and
throughout, Lukács appears crudely to confuse violent experience with historical process, to find in history an objective,

virtually tangible structure that can be uncovered by following "correct" procedures. History, in brief, is equated with
sociology, just as the aesthetics of the novel are also equated
with sociology. A deficient stylist, Lukács doubles back upon
himself, executing drunken transitions and logic-defying
leaps; his aesthetic of the novel, hinted at in numerous chapters throughout *Der historische Roman,* is most lucidly set
forth when he writes that "A close familiarity with the life of
a people is the precondition for real literary invention. In
later bourgeois literature the writer's alienation from the
people is mirrored . . . in two ways: on the one hand, in his
anxious clinging to the facts of contemporary (or historical)
life; on the other, in his conception of artistic invention which
he sees not as the highest literary form of a correct reflection
of objective reality but as something purely subjective which
draws him arbitrarily away from the sole truth of the factual."
And again, "A truthful conception of reality and active parti-
cipation in events constitute for most writers an insoluble
dilemma. How is this dilemma to be solved? Obviously
through life itself, through a writer's connection with the life
of the people. The writer who is deeply familiar with the tendencies at work in popular life, who experiences them as if
they were his own, will feel himself to be simply the execu-
tive organ of these tendencies, his rendering of reality will
appear to him as simply a reproduction of these tendencies
themselves, even should he render every individual fact
differently from the way he found it. 'French society should be
the historian, I but its secretary,' says Balzac." [4]

Lukács' entire system, which is subtler than brief discussion can establish, depends upon his sense of "reality" as
deriving from fidelity to popular life. Such ideological realism
is the sole conductor of truth in fiction. It is a view that leads
to curious literary judgments, beginning with an overvalua-

tion of Scott, who for all his usefulness to intellectual history
was a seriously flawed writer, and it leads to inflation of the
virtues of those writers who confirm Marxian prejudice:
Maxim Gorky, Stefan Zweig, Heinrich Mann, Lion Feucht-
wanger. Aesthetic judgment so far off the mark as Lukács'
implies that other areas of his thought are also suspect, since
aesthetics do not exist *in vacuo*.

Views of history are as numerous as viewers, but something of what I intend by the word "history" is expressed, not
by Lukács, but by Ortega, when he writes that "Man has no
nature. What he has is . . . history"; [5] and by Unamuno, who
says that "History is what God thinks, the process of His
thinking." [6] These are not definitions; rather they may suggest
an aura, a frame of mind, the fertile environment of definition. In a preliminary way, I would regard history, narrowly
and parochially with respect to fiction, as an area of human
experience made available to art, particularly to the new art
of fiction, by the theorists of Romanticism: Herder, Friedrich
Schlegel, Adam Müller, Schiller, Fichte, Schelling, and
Hegel. Scott should be added to the list, not for Lukács' reasons, but because, as Trevelyan wrote of him, Scott's historical intuitions "charged the mind of Europe and taught it
history." [7] Lukács finds Romanticism always "reactionary," [8]
while he finds in Scott "above all, . . . a renunciation of
Romanticism, a conquest of Romanticism, a higher development of the realist tradition of the Enlightenment in keeping
with the new times." [9] The author of *Guy Mannering* and
Ivanhoe might himself be astonished at such a statement.

That area of experience made available to art by Romanticism, then, includes political and social events. It may include exposition of an ideology, but it is not confined by
ideology, nor is the writer an ideologue. History gave scope
and resonance to the novel, qualities that we may distinguish
more clearly in post-Romantic writers than in the exploratory

work of an *echt*-Romantic such as Scott. I have accordingly linked Hermann Broch and Robert Musil in this chapter and the next for a variety of reasons, and despite the fact that from many points of view they may seem to be diametrically opposed in their methods and procedures as novelists.

Broch, the writer who said that neither he nor Musil nor Kafka had a biography—they did nothing but write their books [10]—assuredly kept himself out of most of his prose fiction. Particularly in *Die Schlafwandler* (*The Sleepwalkers*), Broch goes to considerable lengths to contrive the illusion of objectivity and impersonality. His trilogy is by turns dramatic, expressionistic, surreal, and abstract, but throughout it is by intention and achievement firmly historical. Musil, on the other hand, writes almost totally out of his own experience in *Der Mann ohne Eigenschaften* (*The Man without Qualities*). Even if we knew nothing about Musil's life, we would sense in the style, in the voice of Ulrich, and in the events of Ulrich's fictional biography that Ulrich's cavalry service, for one example, was Musil's, and that Ulrich's ironic detachment, his tics and traits, are a mirror-reflection of Robert Musil's. In fact, such superficial polarities merely conceal underlying and fundamental resemblances between the two writers.

It is not accidental that Proust's great novel, *À la recherche du temps perdu*, is literally great, *grand*, huge in extent. It makes inordinate demands upon our time and attention. Proust's own obsessions virtually have to become ours, and as the critic said of Joyce's *Ulysses*, we cannot read it, we can only reread it. Exactly the same is true of Broch's work and of Musil's. They are huge, relentless, and however entertaining and delightful, we come away exhausted, but exalted, stretched beyond a reasonable assumption of what our limit might be.

Richard Blackmur had thoughts about the vastness of

certain modern novels. He proposed that vastness, bulk, has to do with the breakdown between artist and audience: "Because there is too much for the artist to do and too little for the audience to bring, there is a failure of relation between the artist and his art and between the art and its audience." That breakdown, Blackmur wrote, was Joyce's theme, as it was Thomas Mann's and Marcel Proust's. I would not hesitate to add Broch and Musil to the list. Blackmur continued in an essay on Joyce, "Taking *Ulysses* as a characteristic example of the novel into which the breakdown has forced itself as theme, we see at once how the artist has on the one hand been compelled to take a series of arbitrary aesthetic, technical, and intellectual measures to get his work moving and has on the other hand been required, in order to fill out these measures, to present an inordinate mass of detail. He is arbitrary because what would formerly have been authorities have become part of his subject-matter, and he is omnivorous of detail because without his authorities he has no principles of economy." [11]

I think there is much truth in Blackmur's view, although I cannot share his belief in "failure between the artist and his art." Blackmur's statement further provides a link to the matter in the preceding chapter concerning historical Romanticism, post-Romanticism, and the Romantic writer's quasi-scientific concern for fact, for detail, *in* nature, and, one might add, *apart* from nature. Proust's vastness in part reflects his almost transcendental awareness of the natural world, together with an implied faith that through nature lies salvation, but only when allied to art, to the narrator's ultimate perception of the work that he must write.

One has only to look at shelves of prose fiction arranged chronologically to perceive the fact of vastness as a function of eighteenth-century sensibility and of Romanticism. Many exceptions such as *Don Quixote* exist, but in the main, the *contes*, tales, and epistolary novels of the seventeenth and eighteenth centuries are brief, pithy, and direct—Classical, if you will. Manners and convention served those writers well, together with at least the shared illusion of the presence of those forces that one could once refer to, without irony, as culture and civilization. But when Samuel Richardson discovered, or uncovered, the new mode of sensibility, he needed a huge number of pages for the construction of *Pamela, Clarissa,* and *Sir Charles Grandison.* Twenty years after having written *Wilhelm Meisters Lehrjahre,* Goethe returned to his theme in *Wilhelm Meisters Wanderjahre.* The characteristic Romantic novel, whether historical, contemporary, or *Bildungsroman,* was vast in extent. Realism and Naturalism, movements that are supposed to have superseded Romanticism, may be seen as refinements upon Romanticism, even in the crude measure of size. Naturalism in particular, with its emphasis on detail, its faith that precision and fullness of observation will render scientific truth, simply provided one further rationalization for the earlier Romantic turn of mind, in which the writer needed to create all the circumstances of his work, unwilling or unable to trust to conventional formulas. The novelist became in effect surveyor, road builder, manufacturer of the vehicle, and driver, too. Such is nowhere more true than in the United States, where the typical best seller still runs to five hundred or more pages.

Both Broch and Musil stood directly in the post-Romantic line, then, where size was concerned; and when one says size, one is of course alluding to form. Neither solved the problem of form, but each writer's monumental assault upon the problem, however one may fault it, is far more interesting and valuable than many a lesser writer's success. Broch fascin-

ates through paradox. The most relentlessly intellectual of
writers, he despaired of rationality. "Der Rationalismus," he
wrote in an unpublished note, "ist etwas Begrenzendes,
Begrenztes. . . ." [12] ("Rationality is limiting and limited. . . .")
He despaired of art, too, but he tried to link art to a rational
philosophy, to get away from his conviction of the limitations
of rationality through the art of the novel. Broch has been
characterized with fair accuracy as *Dichter wider Willen*,[13] a
writer in spite of himself. In his essays and to a degree in his
fiction, he struggled to impose an impossible unity upon
philosophy, natural science, mathematics, art, and society.
Born in 1886, Broch was twenty-eight when World War I
began; he was arrested as a Jew in 1938 thanks to the Nazi
occupation of Austria, but he was permitted to emigrate to
Britain and ultimately to the United States following the intervention of friends, among them James Joyce.[14] Thus knowing
at first hand the outrages of contemporary history, Broch
wanted to discard the merely aesthetic. He was impatient and
satirical about the efforts of modern writers to project self at
the expense of total context; art alone was not enough.

In 1947, Broch wrote of Kafka, "He reached the point
of the Either-Or: either poetry is able to proceed to myth, or
it goes bankrupt. Kafka, in his presentiment of the new cos-
mogony, the new theogony that he had to achieve, struggling
with his love for literature, his disgust for literature, feeling
the ultimate insufficiency of any artistic approach, decided
(as did Tolstoy, faced with a similar decision) to quit the realm
of literature, and asked that his work be destroyed; he asked
this for the sake of the universe whose new mythical concept
had been bestowed upon him." [15] Further to his attack upon
mere aesthetics, Broch set up a Kantian opposition between
the terms *Erkenntnis* and *Bekenntnis*.[16] *Bekenntnis* is mere
knowledge of self, that knowledge attained through narcis-

sistic self-contemplation and through confession. *Erkenntnis,* for Broch, took on a quality transcending its common definition: knowledge of the world beyond the self, objective knowledge. For him it also meant intuition of that objective, unified world, which Broch often expressed in the language of the Platonic dialogues.[17] "Self-knowledge is nothing; intuitive knowledge is everything," [18] he wrote; and again, concerning Joyce, "immer ist Dichten eine Ungeduld der Erkenntnis." [19] This last is untranslatable, but a free rendering might read, "composition is always a compromise with intuited truth." Broch, in short, like many a Romantic before him, was a religious man without religion, a visionary who took upon himself the task of reconciling not just opposites but also the profoundly antagonistic elements in the world he found about him. He longed for a world system, for unity, for regeneration through inspired rationality, for salvation.

It was in *Die Schlafwandler* and only in that novel, I think, that Broch found the balance he sought between *Bekenntnis* and *Erkenntnis,* between intuition and observation, between apocalypse and salvation. Before examining that novel, however, it may be profitable to survey what Broch thought he was about in the area of fiction. His ideas are most clearly expressed in his lecture on James Joyce, and in the published essay. Broch delivered the lecture in 1932, on the occasion of Joyce's fiftieth birthday, and shortly after the completion of the third and final volume of *Die Schlafwandler.* Like many another novelist turned critic, Broch uses *Ulysses* as an echo chamber of his own ideas and preconceptions about art and the place of art in some ideal schema of human life. He admires Joyce for escaping from the merely personal, from *Bekenntnis,* to the expression of an epoch. To make that leap is "a mythical task, mythical in the secret of its action, mythical in its emergence into exterior form, in its shaping

into symbols of the secret forces of chaos, mythical in per-
formance and as influence." [20]

Broch welcomes what he interprets as absence of rationality in Joyce, and he is highly enthusiastic about the symbolic
and the "allegorical" (his word) intent of the narrative. Symbol
and allegory contribute to "Totalität," to the construction of
an essentially Platonic concept: "It is a question of the Platonic ideality of events, the simultaneity of which is determined from the I, and only from the I, from an I that in this
particular case is named Bloom, but finally the I directly, that
is, directly human." [21] Broch goes on to set up an elaborate
parallel between the problems of the novel, the difficulty of
attaining an ideal universality, and the problems of painting
and music, using his terms more or less interchangeably. He
wants, in short, to place Joyce firmly in the modern tradition,
whose most typical representative, he says, is Picasso.[22]
Broch quotes Wittgenstein to the effect that the most burning
questions of our time are not accessible to logic, but must be
posed in the language of mysticism.[23]

Broch's Hegelian emphasis upon simultaneity of past and
contemporary event, his insistence upon a carefully enunciated philosophical system, his discovery in Joyce of certain of
his favorite ideas and methods, are a good indication of the
ground that he had covered in his recently completed trilogy.
The language of the essay, like the language of the novel, is
peculiarly charged with ethical meaning: his central and
recurrent terms in the essay are those of the novel, and they
are those of the conscious life, one cannot doubt. They
include *Erschütterung* (agitation, violent emotion), *Cynicis-
mus, Pessimismus, animalisch, rational, irrational, Totalität,
Modernität, Universalität, Wertauflösung* (dissolution of
values), *logisch, Verantwortung* (responsibility), *Ethik.* As
essayist, and to a degree as novelist, Broch longed for exter-

ior support, from Plato, Kant, and a wide range of modern philosophers; from sociology and from history. He engaged in a
kind of intellectual synaesthesia, a mingling of modes that
suggests his lingering Romanticism of the soft, pejorative variety, a mode in which one form appears, or is made to appear,
as though it fulfills the demands of another. Broch's apparently disciplined notion of the necessity for a new order often
disguises a nostalgia for the past, however ironically presented; and it reveals a familiar figure in our literature, the
writer struggling either to evade or to extend the only tradition immediately available to him, that of Romanticism.

Die Schlafwandler is nothing if not a vision of history, yet
it is not historical in the textbook sense of the word. Broch
wrote to his publisher that "The day of the poly-historical
novel has dawned. . . . It is absolute Kitsch to consider that
the novel is literature having to do with the basic motives of
the soul, or that it can convey to the reader an "organized"
social message." [24] A single narrative in the traditional mode
oversimplifies in that it suggests one answer, one insight; by
poly-historical, Broch describes the irrationality of history,
and the necessity for the writer to convey the true complexity
of existence. Broch uses history, then, and his perceptions
have the objective truth of history, insofar as history can be
said to have objective truth; but his method is to project a set
of imaginative intuitions, both analytical and prophetic, of
German history from 1888 to 1918, dates that he carefully
supplies in the titles of the volumes of the trilogy: 1888:
Pasenow oder die Romantik; 1903: Esch oder die Anarchie;
and 1918: Huguenau oder die Sachlichkeit.[25] The novel provides us with a psychological and philosophical account of
German society in the years before World War I, together with
a harrowing, although indirect, account of that war. Die
Schlafwandler is prophetic in that it anticipates and explains,

however "ambiguously," [26] the rise of Nazism and the Thousand-Year Reich.

Where Proust arrived only finally, at the conclusion of his long work, at a vision of history, Broch and Musil too began with a vision of history. Their progress, nevertheless, through their long works was such that they concluded by having taken a kind of Proustian journey in reverse. This is not to suggest Proustian influence, nor that Broch and Musil were in any tangible sense Proustian. It is rather to reaffirm the workings of history in three writers of post-Romantic sensibility.

The Romantic of the first volume of *Die Schlafwandler* is not an abstraction; he is Joachim, younger son of old Pasenow, a *Junker* of Mark Brandenburg, mindless but foxy, having the manners and outlook of a *Spiesser* (petit-bourgeois), together with the arrogance of the landed gentry. From the outset, Broch might appear to the unwary to write as a naturalist of the historical period of the novel. But soon it is apparent that his Romantic is also a "sleepwalker," that recurrent image that turns up both by name and by implication throughout the trilogy. Subtly and almost imperceptibly, the novel becomes expressionistic; the focus is just off, and the balance point of incident or description never quite determined. As younger son, Joachim von Pasenow is destined for the army, even though by temperament his older brother, Helmuth, would be the better candidate. Joachim, however, is obedient, not very intelligent, and every unthinking inch of him is devoted to carrying out the family's plans for his career.

Joachim is presented always in terms of the clothing he wears, Broch seeming to adapt *Sartor Resartus* for us. Joachim's military uniform protects him from the world; it defines his role in life and it is precious to him. As the novel opens, old Pasenow, on his annual visit to Berlin, with its casinos and prostitutes, obliges his son to come along, and in civilian clothes:

Now that Joachim von Pasenow had put on his frock-coat and between the two corners of his peaked stiff collar his chin was enjoy-
ing unaccustomed freedom, now that he had fixed on his curly-
brimmed top-hat and picked up his walking-stick with a pointed ivory
crook handle, now that he was on the way to the hotel to take out
his father for the obligatory evening's entertainment, suddenly
Eduard von Bertrand's image rose before him, and he felt glad his
civilian clothes did not sit on him with by any means the same
inevitability as on that gentleman, whom in secret he sometimes
thought of as a traitor.[27]

Although this is early on, already the elusive Bertrand is
present, described here as a traitor, later to assume his role
of seducer, should he so desire, of Pasenow's fiancée, Elisabeth von Baddensen. Throughout the first volume Bertrand
is the anti-Romantic, the spokesman for rationality in the
midst of irrational and outmoded Prussian codes of thought
and behavior. Immediately after the first dramatic incident
of the novel, the night at the casino and Joachim von Pasenow's
meeting with the prostitute Ruzena, Broch abruptly — expres-
sionistically — shifts to Bertrand, or rather to Bertrand's mind,
for we have not yet met him in the flesh:

On the theme of the military uniform Bertrand could have sup-
plied some such theory as this:
Once upon a time it was the Church alone that was exalted as
judge over mankind, and every layman knew that he was a sinner.
Nowadays it is the layman who has to judge his fellow-sinner if all
values are not to fall into anarchy, and instead of weeping with him,
brother must say to brother: "You have done wrong." And as once it
was only the garments of the priest that marked a man off from his
fellows as something higher, some hint of the layman peeping through
even the uniform and robe of office, so, when the great intolerance
of faith was lost, the secular robe of office had to supplant the sacred
one, and society had to separate itself into secular hierarchies with
secular uniforms and invest these with the absolute authority of a
creed. And because, when the secular exalts itself as the absolute,

the result is always romanticism, so the real and characteristic romanticism of that age was the cult of the uniform, which implied, as it
were, a superterrestrial and supertemporal idea of uniform, an idea
which did not really exist and yet was so powerful that it took hold
of men far more completely than any secular vocation could, a nonexistent and yet so potent idea that it transformed the man in uniform into a property of his uniform, and never into a professional
man in the civilian sense; and this perhaps simply because the man
who wears the uniform is content to feel that he is fulfilling the most
essential function of his age and therefore guaranteeing the security
of his own life. [P. 20.]

This is just one fragment of a long meditation which manages to combine historical accuracy, a kind of horror, and
comedy, as Broch shifts the point of view from Bertrand to a
reported interior monologue that must be associated with Joachim von Pasenow. Now the meditation concerns the comfort
that a soldier may take in the fact that his uniform provides a
hard casing against whatever is "soft and flowing" in the human body. Just as the wearer, braced with straps and belts,
can forget his own underclothing, so he is no longer tied to
wife or child; "and as things scarcely concern him any longer
he is able to divide them into good and bad, for on intolerance
and lack of understanding the security of life is based" (p. 20).

But it is Bertrand, or what Bertrand might have said, that
directs us to the theme of history, to Broch's first meditation on
history, and one that he frequently repeats in his third volume.
The history recounted is a lament, for when religious authority
is lost, Broch says, when "the secular exalts itself as the
absolute, the result is always romanticism": a Romanticism
Platonic in outline by which the uniform takes the place of an
idea that did not really exist, but which transformed a man
"into a property of his uniform." Men, that is, play a role for
which no lines have been written; role-playing figures large
in Broch's mind and in his novel. Characters will change

roles from volume to volume. Parenthetically, I wonder whether Broch had in mind Julien Sorel of *Le Rouge et le noir* when he wrote of "some hint of the layman peeping through even the uniform and robe of [priestly] office." One recalls Julien's priestly cassock under which the scarlet of his uniform shines, giving Stendhal his title.

In his role as obedient son, Joachim von Pasenow courts Elisabeth von Baddensen, at his father's urging; the old man wants to join the properties of the two families. Joachim actually loves Ruzena, the Bohemian prostitute whom his father had tried to buy for him at the Jäger Casino. Joachim can court Ruzena only in civilian clothes, however; fumblingly, although successfully, like a sleepwalker, Broch writes, and filled with puritanical guilt. Whether involved with Ruzena or courting Elisabeth, Joachim is always put off balance by Bertrand, whether Bertrand in the flesh or the imagined figure who looms disturbingly for him in his conscious mind and in his half-conscious fantasies. The "real" Bertrand has left military service and is a cotton merchant, one who travels to America, to Africa, and other places unsettling to Joachim because they are beyond his ken. It is Bertrand who casts aspersions on the German colonies in Africa, calling them "Romantic" (the British colonies are a better investment), and it is Bertrand who cynically questions the point of Joachim's brother's death. Helmuth has been killed in a duel with a Polish landowner, and to the Pasenows their son has died for their honor. Bertrand stands between Ruzena and Joachim by his hardheadedness; he points out that she is not an actress, although Joachim has tried to set her up as such; she shall have a dress shop. That prospect wounds her, together with her suspicion that Joachim seeks Bertrand's approval for his relationship with her. She ineffectually shoots Bertrand, her act anticipating the marvelous scene that will take place between Esch, the central figure, and Bertrand in the second volume, *Esch oder die Anarchie*. Powerfully, even hauntingly, Bertrand stands equivocally between Joachim and Elisabeth, whom old Pasenow, facing death, has ordered Joachim to marry. Elisabeth goes to Bertrand for advice, actually out of love for him, a state which she does not clearly recognize in herself. Bertrand tells her that Joachim, in effect, is too unintelligent to love her; that he, Bertrand, loves her, but that he will not marry her. Wisely, or unwisely, she accepts Joachim.

Throughout all this, Broch constructs with delicate skill an image of poor Joachim von Pasenow as the landed aristocrat lost in empty custom forced upon him by his role as only surviving son of his father. That complex of meaning is never insisted upon directly; rather it is always oblique and virtually invisible. Broch's technique must be observed: After his father's stroke, Joachim goes to Stolpin, the family seat, to look after his father's affairs. He sees Elisabeth a good deal, and we read,

Since the old man's illness, which still kept him in bed the greater part of the day, life had become curiously simplified. Joachim could now reflect more quietly on many things, and some of the riddles appeared less obscure, or at least more approachable. But now an almost insoluble problem confronted him, and it was no use trying to decipher it in Elisabeth's face, for her face itself constituted the problem. Lying back in her chair she was gazing at the autumn landscape, and her up-tilted face, thrown back almost at a right angle to the taut line of the throat, was like an irregular roof set upon the pillar of her neck. One could perhaps say just as well that it rested like a leaf on the calyx of the throat, or that it was a lid covering the throat, for it was really no longer a face, merely a continuation of the throat, an extension from the throat, with a far-off resemblance to the head of a serpent. Joachim followed the line of her throat; the chin jutted out like a hill, behind which lay the landscape of her face.

Softly rounded the rim of the crater which was her mouth, dark the
cavern of the nose, divided by a white pillar. Like a miniature beard
sprouted the hedge of the eyebrows, and beyond the clearing of the
forehead, cut by finely ploughed furrows, was the edge of the forest.
[P. 106.]

Nothing answers Joachim's question as to how a woman can
be desirable. It remains "insoluble and perplexing" to him.

After the shooting incident, after Joachim has paid off
Ruzena, he comes around to asking Baron von Baddensen for
Elisabeth's hand. He then confronts her, and we read, "while
Joachim was still trying to find the right words he heard Elisabeth say almost gaily: 'So you want to marry me, Joachim;
have you thought it over carefully?'" (P. 140.) This strikes
Joachim as "undamenhaft" (unladylike), and he further reflects that it might almost have been Bertrand speaking. He
cannot decide whether to get down on one knee or not. The
piece of furniture on which he is sitting is so low that he
might be construed already to be on one knee. He asks if he
might venture to hope? Then,

Elisabeth made no answer; she had thrown her head back, and her
eyes were half shut. As he now gazed at her face he was disquieted
to find that a section of landscape could be transferred within four
walls; it was the very memory he had feared, it was that noonday
under the autumn trees, it was that blending of contours, and he
almost wished that the Baron's consent had been longer postponed.
For more dreadful than a brother's apparition in a woman's face is
the landscape that luxuriates over it, landscape that takes posses-
sion of it and absorbs the dehumanized features, so that not even
Helmuth could avail to arrest their undulating flow. [P. 140.]

A disjointed conversation between the two odd lovers
follows, in which each is really talking to, or about, the absent
Bertrand. Elisabeth of Bertrand's love, or lack of love for her;

Joachim of Bertrand as tempter, himself as Elisabeth's savior. Joachim has not expressed himself well,

what he wanted to say, for what he expected from God and from Elisabeth was not a mere equivalent for Christian family life as he had been trained to understand it; yet just because he expected more from Elisabeth, he desired to confine his words to the neighbour-hood of that celestial sphere in which she was to manifest herself as the tenderest of silvery, hovering Madonnas. Perhaps she would have to die before she could speak to him in the right way, for as she sat there leaning back, she looked like Snow-white in the glass casket and was so irradiated by that higher beauty and heavenly essence that her face had but little resemblance to the one he had known in life before it blended so dreadfully and irrevocably with the land-scape. [Pp. 141–142.]

They continue their curious conversation, describing death, Bertrand's death, which is confused for Joachim with his father, with Helmuth, his dead brother, and with a vision of Elisabeth in death.

The novel ends on their wedding night, with Joachim frantically uncomfortable in his wife's room, placing the candles so that she will look like Snow White, and offering her her "freedom" before the prospect of her "sacrifice." Instead of a sign from God, Joachim hears Bertrand's words in Elisa-beth's mouth, "like a Mephistophelean sign from the demon and the Evil One." When at length Elisabeth coaxes Joachim near her and tries to coax him in, Broch reverts to the subject of clothing:

She had moved a little to the side, and her hand, which with its befrilled wrist was all that emerged from the bedclothes, rested in his. Through his position his military coat had become disordered, the lapels falling apart left his black trousers visible, and when Joachim noticed this he hastily set things right again and covered the place. He had now drawn up his legs, and so as not to touch the sheets with his patent-leather shoes, he rested his feet in a rather constrained posture on the chair standing beside the bed. [P. 158.]

Through thematic repetition and through his use of imagery and leitmotif, Broch performs a variety of tasks which the novelist, as Broch understands his own undertaking, must perform: he removes the naturalistic curse of typicality from his Joachim and his Elisabeth, while his allusive expressionism and symbolism keep steadily in focus his historical intention. Not least, Broch reaches a level of wild, ponderous, unlikely comedy in his portrayal of Joachim and his beloved uniform, as he will do later of Esch and his erotic confusions. Such comedy is essential, for it anchors the novel in human reality and again removes the incipient danger of excessive fantasy. Broch is not a witty writer, but he is comic, and his kind of comedy, like Kafka's, is poised on the fine line from which it may readily topple over into tragedy.

Pasenow oder die Romantik, like many episodes in Broch's second volume, then, is undeniably comic. Repeatedly, Broch uses the word "Romantik" derisively and makes continual fun of Joachim. How, one must ask, does Broch as comedian (to say nothing of Musil) square with any definition of Romanticism, whether historical or post-Romantic? We assume, properly I think, that the detachment and objectivity necessary to comedy are attributes of Classicism. We do not go to the classical works of Romanticism for amusement. No recent critic has treated that apparent paradox more convincingly than Morse Peckham in an article of 1951. It will save time to turn aside from Broch long enough to notice Peckham's approach.

Peckham remarks that conventional theories of Romanticism have no difficulty in accounting for historical, full-blown Romanticism, but that such theories encounter heavy going when they confront certain writers or certain kinds of obstreperous writings labeled Romantic. Such theories cannot account for Byron or for Byronic themes, for Byronic rejection of values which a mature Wordsworth would accept; for Byron's irony, his satire, or for his dramatic objectivity in *Don Juan.* Peckham's term "negative Romanticism" to account for Byron is probably more precise and satisfactory than the conventional but vague "pre-Romantic," or suggestions that Byron was really a misplaced eighteenth-century wit who had strayed into the nineteenth century. Peckham writes that "negative romanticism is the expression of the attitudes, the feelings, and the ideas of a man who has left static mechanism but has not yet arrived at a reintegration of his thought and art in terms of dynamic organicism." [28] Peckham identifies the Coleridge of the *Ancient Mariner,* the Wordsworth of *The Prelude,* and the Carlyle of *Sartor Resartus* as writers in the stage of negative Romanticism. For them it is a temporary period, their *Sturm und Drang,* a preliminary to positive Romanticism. "The typical symbols of negative romanticism are individuals who are filled with guilt, despair, and cosmic and social alienation. They are often presented . . . as having committed some horrible and unmentionable crime in the past. They are often outcasts from men and God. . . . They are Harolds, . . . Manfreds, they are Cains. They are the heroes of such poems as *Alastor.* But when they begin to get a little more insight into their position, as they are forced to develop historical consciousness, as they begin to seek the sources for their negation and guilt and alienation, they become Don Juans. That is, in *Don Juan,* Byron sought objectivity by means of satire, and set out to trace in his poem the development of those attitudes that had resulted in himself . . . positive romanticism cannot explain Byron, but negative romanticism can. Byron spent his life in the situation of Wordsworth after the rejection of Godwin and before his move to Racedown and Nether Stowey, of the Mariner alone on the wide, wide sea, of Teufelsdröckh subject to the Everlasting No and wandering through the Centre of Indifference." [29]

In a later article (1961) on the same subject, Peckham goes to the familiar idea that Romanticism is marked by the separation of the role from the self, but that "With the collapse of the Enlightenment there also collapses the natural social structure, and with it the possibility of playing a role. Hence the social alienation which accompanies the cosmic alienation, or loss of relatedness to the perceived world. The first step at reconstituting value, then, is to strip bare the self, or more accurately, to invent the self, to conceptualize the sense of identity." [30]

Are we not here at the very center of Broch's, and Musil's, effort? Pasenow, Esch, and Huguenau, Broch's three central figures, in their different ways, are in process of trying to perceive the collapse, incipient or already accomplished, of the social structure, and trying—through blind allegiance to tradition, in the case of Pasenow; through a mystique of justice and pneumatic bliss in a featherbed with Mutter Hentjen, in the case of Esch; through thrusting his way out of war service, with detours for robbery, rape, and murder, into the postwar brotherhood of the *Spiesser*, in the case of Huguenau—to achieve insight into themselves, into history, and to bring themselves back into history from their frightening isolation. As for technique, Broch's objectivity and intellectual control are distinctly related to the conception of negative Romanticism. They are also related to the German tradition of romantic irony, for Broch as writer remains above his material, controlling it, out of it as narrator or character, yet inevitably of it and in it.

Another view of such matters emerges if one remembers

Joyce and Broch's repeatedly declared admiration for *Ulysses*. Both *Ulysses* and *Die Schlafwandler* are novels of the human conscience, of conscience functioning apart from its base in either a theological or a viable social order. In Leopold Bloom's confusion, Broch may well have found his own great theme, confusion itself. Broch's central figures constitute modern man as sacrificial victim, deluded actor, and ironic-tragic figure in the dissolution of a world. Broch may also have been indebted to *Ulysses* for his treatment of sex, a portion of which I have noted with respect to Pasenow and Elisabeth. In *Die Schlafwandler* sex is neither romantic, tragic, nor naturalistic, although it owes something to all three modes. Like Joyce (Plumtree's potted meat), Broch perceives the comic possibilities of sex, but he also has a "scientific" view of sex which yet escapes the mechanical or the clinical. This is particularly clear in *Esch oder die Anarchie*. August Esch, the "perfekter Buchhalter," the perfect bookkeeper whose motto "business is business" is no protection against his dismissal as part of a plan to conceal a superior's shady work, this Esch sees the world through an opacity even thicker than Pasenow's. Esch spends his days after he has been sacked wandering about Mannheim, guilty and paranoid, given to visions, confusions, and plots for getting into Mutter Hentjen's bed. And one recalls the sequence in which the theatrical producer, Teltscher, introduces Esch to Ruzena, Pasenow's true love in volume I, and now a flower in Teltscher's bouquet of lady wrestlers, bearing the name "The Lioness of Bohemia." Broch at once removes the parody-cliché associations which he deliberately evoked in the person of Ruzena in the first volume and brings into different focus Pasenow's early confusions, now confounded in the mind of Esch. Pasenow does not appear in *Esch oder die Anarchie*, but he is unquestionably present in the person of Ruzena, all of which is at once comic and disturbing.

Esch is attracted sexually to the juggler's beautiful
accomplice, Ilona; he goes to the theater to see her turn. She
wears spangled tights, she moves with grace, uttering short
cries, ultimately to be "crucified" on a heavy backboard. She
assumes her position of crucifixion, the juggler-knife thrower
"bent his body back and now it was he who sent out the dis-
cordant exotic cry, while the dagger flew whistling from his
hand, whizzed straight across the stage, and quivered in the
black wood with a dull impact beside the body of the crucified
girl" (p. 179). The air is filled with whizzing daggers, and
"Esch could almost have wished that it was himself who was
standing up there with his arms raised to heaven, that it was
himself being crucified, could almost have wished to station
himself in front of that gentle girl and receive in his own
breast the menacing blades; and had the juggler, as often
happened, asked whether any gentleman in the audience
would deign to step on to the stage and place himself against
the black board, in sober truth Esch would have accepted the
offer" (pp. 179–180). Disguising to himself the sexual symbolism at work through his vision of himself as Christ crucified, Esch anticipates his preoccupation with religion in the
final volume, together with his own murder at the hands of
Huguenau fifteen years later. In all its evoked meanings, the
episode is a triumph of Broch's art, and a vindication of the
expressionist-cum-surrealist impulse in post-Romantic prose
fiction.

All the more so is the portrait of Bertrand in *Esch oder die
Anarchie*, where again the dominant overtone is sexual, even
while Broch brings together virtually all the themes of the
trilogy. The Bertrand of *The Anarchist* is no longer, as he was
in *The Romantic*, the hardheaded anti-Romantic, the measure of current historical reality in a society bent upon denying
the present. He is still in business as director of the shipping
firm for which Esch had been bookkeeper. Now Bertrand is

impalpable, presented to us through the fog of Esch's para-
noia as a homosexual, and a god-like figure who at once reflects
Esch's feelings of guilt and appears to judge them. In perhaps
the finest episode that Broch ever wrote, Esch makes his way
from Mannheim along the Rhine to Bertrand's lodge, not
neglecting to send a postcard from Müllheim for Mutter
Hentjen's collection. After moving like a sleepwalker through
a maze of rooms, Esch finds, or thinks that he finds, Bertrand,
who is "clean-shaven like an actor, and yet was not an actor"
(p. 298), a recurrence of the idea of Bertrand as actor first
suggested in *Pasenow oder die Romantik.* Esch will murder
Bertrand; Esch feels a rush of love for Bertrand. Esch would
rationalize Bertrand's death through the imprisonment of
Esch's friend, Martin. "But Bertrand, who evidently understood everything, seemed to understand this too, though his
voice, more serious now, still kept its tone of reassuring and
light gaiety: 'But Esch, how can anybody be so cowardly?
Does one need a pretext for a murder?' " (P. 299.) After this,
which anticipates by a decade and more the fictional center
of Sartre's and Camus's best work in the genre, the "dialogue" between Esch and Bertrand culminates in Bertrand's
"Many must die, many must be sacrificed, so that a path may
be prepared for the loving redeemer and judge. And only
through his sacrificial death can the world be redeemed to a
new innocence. But first the Antichrist must come—the mad
and dreamless Antichrist. First the world must become quite
empty, must be emptied of everything in it as by a vacuum
cleaner—nothingness." (P. 301.) Broch's mad mixture here of
Dostoevsky and Lewis Carroll is entirely appropriate to his
interpretation of political and social events in Germany in
the years before World War I. In terms of the construction of
the trilogy, the scene anticipates the entire freight of meaning of volume III, *Hugenau oder die Sachlichkeit* and speci-

fically the ambiguous final pages of that volume, Broch's prophetic anticipation, as I read it, of the Third Reich.

That most interesting confrontation between Esch and Bertrand, a culmination of Broch's art as novelist, forces upon our attention a quality of post-Romantic fiction prominent in German and American writers in particular: that tendency of the symbolic novel (the novel of history is often symbolic) to become mythic, archetypal. The *Joseph* novels of Thomas Mann, together with *Doktor Faustus*, come first to mind, but in *Die Schlafwandler* we have a perhaps more pertinent example. Again Joyce's *Ulysses* might have provided the model or the authority for the classical parallel, or parody. G. C. Schoolfield has read *Die Schlafwandler* as a detailed counterpart to the *Aeneid* and to the life and work of Saint Paul.[31] The thesis is ingenious, and in its details it may be unconvincing: it is hard to see both Ruzena and Mutter Hentjen as Dido, or Bertrand as both Turnus and Apollo. For evidence, Schoolfield says that Apollo was the god of shipping, Bertrand's business; that Bertrand has long hair, and is musical. Esch as Aeneas and as Saint Paul, because of Esch's conversion, may be equally hard to accept in Broch's context. The maze of rooms through which Esch makes his way to his interview with Bertrand is the maze at Cumae, and Cumae symbolizes divine impregnability, in that Esch does not kill Bertrand; their confrontation is that between Aeneas and the god.

Such a reading may finally be unconvincing because Schoolfield does not take into account the literary mode of Broch's presentation: neither the surrealist or expressionistic aspect, nor his humor, nor his historical intent. The parallel with the *Aeneid* is present, I think, but playfully, like Joyce's parallel to the *Odyssey*, which playfulness conceals a trap for the unwary. Parody is also present, a parody that may remind us again of Richard Blackmur's words about artist, work, and audience. The temptation to archetype and myth is particularly strong to a writer like Broch, because it offers an evasion of time and an easy way around history, a temptation powerful to a writer who disdained art, who placed philosophical absolutes foremost, but whose first impulse and commanding talent was for the art of the novel. Surrealism, above all, is dangerous in that by definition it distorts time and liberates, if that is the word, the writer from what he might regard as his first duty, a duty to his vision of history. Broch's own vision of history may be less visionary if we see it, in the chapter to follow, in the perspective of Musil's work.[32]

CHAPTER 3

Robert Musil

It is impossible to deal with Robert Musil's great, unfinished novel, *Der Mann ohne Eigenschaften* (*The Man without Qualities*) without at least mentioning the textual difficulties involved in the publication and translation of Musil's various manuscripts. Because those textual problems are almost Oriental in complexity, they influence one's conception of what Musil really wrote, in which sequence, and where his major points of emphasis belong. No other modern text with which I am familiar presents such formidable impediments. The standard German text is that edited by Adolf Frisé and published by Rowohlt in Hamburg in 1952; it forms the basis of the only English translation, that of Ernst Kaiser and Eithne Wilkins (who have since become Kaiser and Kaiser, a union that might have given Musil a wry satisfaction).[1] Upon his death in Geneva in 1942, Musil left approximately half the work in a confused state of drafts in various stages of completion, to the degree that any editor was fated to have a difficult job on his hands. According to the vast researches of Wilhelm Bausinger, the Kaisers,[2] and the scholars of the Vereinigung Robert-Musil-Archiv at Klagenfurt (Musil's

birthplace), Frisé constructed a text arbitrarily, following
some inner logic of his own, for the latter half of the published material. The Kaisers and others have established that
Frisé also included as canonical matter, early and superseded
versions of extensive portions of the first Rowohlt editions of
1930, 1933, and 1943. Rowohlt has since published correc-
tions in the form of Bausinger's Tübingen dissertation in
1964, but in the meantime the damage had been done.[3] One's
Musil tends to be the Musil of one's first reading, no matter
what later research has turned up by way of emendation.

Musil scholarship is in a state of what promises to be
permanent uproar because of differences in interpretation on
the part of excellent readers who have followed the drama of
the Musil text. The Kaisers, for example, in their *Robert Musil:
Eine Einführung in das Werk* tend to discount Musil's social
satire, his eroticism, and his chapters concerning the criminal
psychopath, Moosbrugger, in favor of a Musil who constructs
a utopia of mystical love, of distance from worldly preoccupation with possessions, and of the dominance of faith and intuitive knowledge over mere rationality. The Kaisers base their
interpretation in large degree upon a psychological reading of
Musil's life, as well as upon ambiguities in the texts that Musil
did not live to sort out. No need to dwell on the possible folly
of psychologizing the writer and thus of misreading his
imaginative work. My own reading is based upon the volumes
that Musil did order during his lifetime, together with a conviction that editors should not publish a writer's notes, drafts,
diaries, and newspaper clippings posthumously unless that
writer made it clear before death that such matter in his judgment was literary and publishable. We have enough, I think,
that is authentically Musil's to go on.

Since textual confusion in *Der Mann ohne Eigenschaften*
is even greater than I have indicated, it might be well to re-

view who Musil's characters are and approximately what they are up to, and what his central themes encompass. The novel is vast, competing with *War and Peace* and various other monsters for the dubious distinction of being the longest ever; we may recall Richard Blackmur's theory of length, bulk, in his essay on Joyce. Musil's bulk, however, is unlike Broch's and certainly unlike any of the naturalistic boredoms on American best-seller lists. Musil's length and breadth is not conveniently divided into volumes I through III, like *Die Schlafwandler;* nor is length in Musil's case a function of the realist's or naturalist's purveying of information out of the pseudo-scientific conviction that in information lies truth. Although the Rowohlt edition weighs two kilograms, although it runs to almost 1700 closely printed pages, the novel does not seem long to read. It lacks plot, melodrama, or any of the neo-Gothic flutings of Beckett's people, up to their ears in garbage. There are no armies in Musil's nights, only an occasional rendezvous with the delicious, nymphomaniacal Bonadea. The novel most certainly does not end, nor even begin to conclude in any aesthetically satisfying manner; Musil, surprised by death at sixty-one, had been in no hurry, believing that he had another twenty years in which to conclude his work.

Why then is it not the great bore that it might seem to be at first, forbidding glance? It is not because of Musil's conception of Ulrich, his central character, the man without qualities who possesses many qualities, either in fact or potentially. The shape of the novel is unliterary, almost antiliterary. It is the shape of Musil's life — I am not psychologizing — it both contains and in an unsettling way *is* the speculation, the shifts, and the searchings of a brilliant, skeptical man of faith, a scientist who doubted science, a rationalist who tested rationality to the point where it broke, not so much to disprove it as to find its limits; and a man of so glittering an intelligence that he makes those highly intelligent men, Proust and Broch, look in comparison like a schoolboy and an occasionally inspired clod, respectively.

First, second, last, and always in Musil's novel there is Ulrich: we never learn his surname—it is withheld "out of consideration for his father." Ulrich is thirty-two, a mathematician by profession whose awareness of confusion in the modern world is such that he abandons attempts to cope with it in a practical way and decides to retire for a year to contemplate, to enjoy, perhaps, the circumstance that he *is* a man without qualities. Ulrich is more central than most central characters; all the secondary characters depend from him as a wasp's nest depends from a tree. Ulrich is our way, our medium for perceiving people and things that surround him; this in spite of the fact that the novel is written in the third person, that we hear the writer's voice often, and that Musil takes pains to establish ironic distance between the character, Ulrich, and us, his readers.

Because of Ulrich, the novel has been called,[4] with a certain accuracy, a kind of *Bildungsroman, Bildung*, however, not in the historically Romantic manner of *Wilhelm Meister*, nor even in the manner of Flaubert in *L'Education sentimentale*, but *Bildung* that is very much post-Romantic: ironic, detached, almost upside-down in the sense that Ulrich is keenly aware of his own situation and of the situation of the world about him. Musil himself noted that he did not want to write the *Bildungsroman* of a person, but rather the *Bildungsroman* of an idea.[5]

Ulrich's world is Austria, 1913, or "Kakania" (from the French nursery expression for excrement), as Musil often identifies it; and the clusters of experience that Musil deals with may be crudely divided into the personal and the social, or public, even though those areas are subtly intertwined throughout the first two books. At the personal and more immediate level is the theme of eroticism, which promptly but by gradations turns into the theme of love. Allied to that is the theme of art, which is broached through the Ulrich-Clarisse-Walter triangle, through the pretentious ravings of Meingast, then leaking over into the social area through the Tuzzi-Diotima-Arnheim alliance and the subsidiary or servants' hall counterpart of Rachel-Soliman. The social and public aspects of the novel include foremost the Collateral Campaign, that brilliant device which allows Musil to range up and down society at will, flicking it here and there, like unserious lightning, or concentrating for long periods and less satirically upon what we might call the industrial-military complex, in the marvelous person of Arnheim, and the even more marvelous person of that leader of men, General Stumm von Bordwehr. Also in the public range of meaning is the Ulrich-Moosbrugger-Clarisse theme. Although Moosbrugger is transparently a symbolic figure from the outset, he also embodies a fully evoked public meaning; he is never the surrealist Bertrand of Broch's *Esch*, nor a mythic demon out of Mann's *Doktor Faustus*.

All Musil's characters, themes, threads, and incidents make up an overriding philosophical theme, the outlines of which are visible in the early volumes, but which fade away into textual difficulties and into death itself, the death of the writer who had not made up his mind about his work, and who by nature may have been incapable of ever resolving in a recognizably literary or philosophical manner the nature of the vision that increasingly preoccupied him. The difficulties of interpreting Musil, that is to say, are formidable. In spite of difficulty, in spite of the incompletion of his work and of the daunting matter of the late manuscripts, *Der Mann ohne*

Eigenschaften is still one of the most superb works we have, and one firmly rooted in a distinctive vision of history.

Where Proust arrived only finally, at the conclusion of his long work, at a vision of history, Broch, and even more directly and obviously, Musil, begin with a vision of history. At first glance Musil's vision seems to be contained, as Conrad's often is or as is the Hardy of *The Dynasts,* at the outset, in a god-like overview of the geographical and meteorological scene in which the events of the work will take place, but as we read into Musil's first paragraph, we are at once in the ample lap of his irony:

> There was a depression over the Atlantic. It was travelling eastwards, towards an area of high pressure over Russia, and still showed no tendency to move northwards around it. The isotherms and isotheres were fulfilling their functions. The atmospheric temperature was in proper relation to the average annual temperature, the temperature of the coldest as well as of the hottest month, and the a-periodic monthly variation in temperature. The rising and setting of the sun and of the moon, the phases of the moon, Venus and Saturn's rings, and many other important phenomena, were in accordance with the forecasts in the astronomical yearbooks. The vapour in the air was at its lowest. In short, to use an expression that describes the facts pretty satisfactorily, even though it is somewhat old-fashioned: it was a fine August day in the year 1913. [I, 3.] [6]

This is masterly. Musil uses the diction of meteorology in such a way as to suggest Paracelsus, or perhaps the Ptolemaic universe, and attempts to predict the future. Time is insisted upon, historical time, and inevitably the World War to come in one calendar year. The fact that the place is Vienna, that much of the action of the Collateral Campaign—the effort properly to celebrate in 1918 the seventieth year of the reign of the Emperor, Franz-Joseph—is directed to the very years of the war, are obvious sources of temporal irony.

The subject of time, Hegelian time, preoccupies the Man without Qualities, as yet nameless, when we are introduced to him in Chapter 2. He stands at the window of his house, watch in hand, counting cars, trams, people passing by:

He was estimating the speed, the angle, the dynamic force of masses being propelled past, which drew the eye after them swift as lightning, holding it, letting it go, forcing the attention—for an infinitesimal instant of time—to resist them, to snap off, and then to jump to the next and rush after that. [I, 7.]

What will the future be like? he wonders. Perhaps the common man (*der Spiessbürger*), flinging himself at his daily tasks,

who has an intuitive prophetic glimpse of the beginning of an immense new, collective, ant-like heroism? It will be called rationalised heroism and will be regarded as very beautiful. But what can we know of that today? However, at that time there were hundreds of such unanswered questions, all of the greatest importance. They were in the air; they were burning underfoot. The time was on the move. People who were not born then will find it difficult to believe, but the fact is that even then time was moving as fast as a cavalry-camel; it is not only nowadays that it does so. But in those days no one knew what it was moving towards. Nor could anyone quite distinguish between what was above and what below, between what was moving forwards and what backwards. [I, 8.]

Temporal confusion depicted through irony disguises prophecy, and veils, for the moment, Musil's temporal framework. The novel is narrated at a timeless moment after the events, even though those events, toward the conclusion, approach inexorably to the narrator's present. The past, that is to say, determines the present moment, which slips away elusively into the future.[7] Musil's novel, as Michael Hamburger has said, is as much about the future as it is about the past.[8] It is thus the reverse of Proustian, although both Proust and Musil were indebted, I suggest, to the Romantic awareness of history and of time.

Just as Broch proposes the subject of history early in *Die Schlafwandler,* so does Musil in *Der Mann ohne Eigenschaften.* Musil broaches it through Ulrich's mental meanderings, glancingly, satirically, now apparently in comedy, now seriously. Of mathematics, Ulrich's profession, we read in the first book:

And so it was that even at that time, when Ulrich became a mathematician, there were people who were prophesying the collapse of European civilisation on the grounds that there was no longer any faith, any love, any simplicity or any goodness left in mankind; and it is significant that these people were all bad at mathematics in school. [I, 41.]

In context, this is important for telling us a good deal about Ulrich's own approach to scientific method. He reflects that people who object to science simply do not know what thought can accomplish; that if they could be taught to think in a new way, they would live in a different manner. Science offers the possibility of regeneration; at the same time, the irony of history is simultaneously evoked and prophesied. History as subject comes up directly, although again through a veil of irony, in the course of the development of the Collateral Campaign.

Ulrich becomes involved in the campaign through a misunderstanding about the Moosbrugger case. Through Ulrich's father's friendship for Count Stallburg, Ulrich is drawn into the notion of somehow commemorating the seventy-year reign of the Emperor and King of Kakania, as opposed to the mere thirty-year reign that Wilhelm II of Germany would enjoy in power by 1918. Like Broch, Musil chooses his dates with care.

Ulrich is sent on to Count Leinsdorf, a mindless Machiavelli, a courtier whose great power derives from his bloodlines and his banking, not from his intelligence. The all-absorbing question is: how shall the nation, the empire, suitably celebrate the fabulous seventieth anniversary? Ulrich reads out Fichte's "Address to the German Nation" to suggest a properly nationalistic idea for the campaign, but Leinsdorf rejects Fichte as anti-Catholic. They have four points to go on, the Count says: Emperor of Peace, European Landmark, True Austria, and Culture and Capital. The rest, he is sure, will take care of itself. In the meantime, there is the salon of a distant cousin of Ulrich's, Ermelinda Tuzzi, wife of Tuzzi, permanent secretary in the Ministry of Foreign Affairs. She is, Ulrich decides, in her lack of a lover, "eine geistige Schönheit" (p. 94), a high-minded beauty, a second Diotima, and Diotima she remains.

Frustrated in her marriage to the chilly, ambitious Tuzzi, Diotima is not so much in love with men, as she is, like her Platonic namesake, in love with ideas. She attracts to her salon, and to the committee that will flesh out Count Leinsdorf's four points, men of all sorts, including Leinsdorf himself, and the intellectual industrialist, Arnheim (modeled on Walther Rathenau), who is admitted to the sacred committee as an advisor, even though he is a German. Leinsdorf, on the evening he meets Arnheim at Diotima's salon, knows himself to be in the heart of culture and capital. He develops his thought in terms that make us think of Hermann Broch on the function of the uniform, and on the parallel function of the Church in the Middle Ages:

His Highness Count Leinsdorf — when he did not happen to be calling them "the true élite" — summed up these two elements, so various in themselves, that intermingled at Diotima's in the term "culture and capital." But he liked even better to think of them in terms of "office," that conception occupying a privileged place in his mind. He held the view that every form of productivity — not only that of a civil servant, but equally that of a factory-worker or a concert-singer — represented an "office." "Everyone," he was accustomed to say, "holds an office in the State — the working-man, the prince, the artisan, all are officials!". . . This idea of "office" was for him the substitute for what Diotima referred to as that unity of religious feeling in all human activities that has been lost since the Middle Ages. [I, 115.]

Leinsdorf and Diotima thus between them combine Colonel Blimp with Novalis' wish that all citizens wear uniform, while all combine to make up an extended exegesis to Joachim von Pasenow's behavior in *Die Romantik.*

Diotima's notions about Austria as a nation are part of Musil's approach to history, too. She thinks of culture, which she invariably calls

"our old Austrian culture." This was an expression that she had learnt to make more and more frequent use of since her ambition had become spiritualised by expansion. What she meant by it was: the beautiful paintings of Velasquez and Rubens that hung in the Imperial museums; the fact that Beethoven had been to all intents and purposes an Austrian; Mozart, Haydn, the Cathedral of St. Stephen, the Burgtheater; the Court ceremonial heavy with the weight of tradition; the Innere Stadt, the district where the smartest *couturiers* and dress-shops of an empire with fifty million inhabitants were crowded together; the tactful demeanour of high officials; Viennese cooking; the aristocracy, which considered itself next to none except the English, and its ancient palaces; the social tone, which was permeated with sometimes genuine, usually sham aestheticism. [I, 115–116.] ·

History is broached in the novel through Diotima and Leinsdorf as a joke; something called "the drama of history" accounts for Diotima's attraction to Arnheim, that financier of whom Musil writes: "People liked listening to him because is was so nice that a man who had so many ideas also had money" (I, 236). (Also, Diotima observes that Arnheim does not look the least bit Jewish.) Leinsdorf's reflections about Austro-Hungarian nationhood are lodged in something called "the historical process." The Count is baffled by the fact that the Empire is both Austro and Hungarian, and all the more unable to reconcile his awareness of the duality in that he detests the Hungarians as much as they detest him. Musil writes:

> It entirely suffices if it is noticed that the mysteries of this dualism (such is the technical expression) are at least as difficult to understand as those of the Trinity; for the historical process more or less everywhere resembles a juridical one, with hundreds of clauses, appendices, compromises and protests, and it is only to this that attention should be drawn. All unsuspectingly the common man lives and dies in the midst of it all, and lucky for him that it is so; for if he were to realise in what a process, what an action, he is involved, with how many lawyers, what costs and motives, he might be driven into persecution mania, whatever country he lived in. Understanding reality is exclusively a matter for the historico-political thinker. For him the present time follows the battle of Mohács or of Lietzen as the entrée follows the soup. He has all the records at his fingertips, and at every moment feels the necessity arising out of the nature of the process. And if, what is more, he is, like Count Leinsdorf, an aristocratic politico-historically trained thinker, whose forefathers, agnates and kindred on the distaff side themselves played their part in the preliminary operations, he can survey the result as a line smoothly ascending. [I, 199–200.]

Here we may readily see a veiled allusion to the situation of Moosbrugger, whose case is under appeal, together with an unveiled criticism of historicism, of the notion that the past does in truth lead in some rational, discernible manner to the present and future. Moosbrugger's case is relevant, and the passage a fine illustration of Musil's method at its most successful, for Moosbrugger represents the irrational, a-historical elements of modern life within the context of the novel. He is first a psychopath, a murderer who is imprisoned and tried for having stabbed a prostitute repeatedly because he believed that she was sneering at him, when in fact she was soliciting him. The case becomes notorious throughout Kakania; surely madness must be the reason for the murder, and the man must be put away in an asylum. Moosbrugger will have none of that. He is insulted at the suggestion that he is mad, and he applauds the prosecution when it manages a cogent point against him. He is antihistorical and irrational.

The great Arnheim, however, who is capable of the most outrageous foolishness, which in turn only Ulrich recognizes, is all *for* history. "Great events," he tells Ulrich, "are always the expression of a general situation" (I, 203). Ulrich invents a test to force discrimination within the "general situation": suppose that a composer of operetta is really a conspirator who proclaims himself president of the world?

> "That is quite impossible!" Herr Dr. Arnheim said earnestly.
> "Such a composer cannot be either a conspirator or a politician. If he were, his genius for light music would be unthinkable. And nothing irrational happens in the history of the world." [I, 203–204.]

This put-down of Hegel through the agency of Arnheim, the great bore, is socially and intellectually satisfying, because Arnheim *is* a bore, and because by now in Musil's narrative we are aware of Moosbrugger and all he stands for, together with the hints and foreshadowings of the mystical, neo-Platonic synthesis that Musil will explicitly work toward later on.

History as a specific theme takes a serious turn in Chapter 83, a surprising turn in its very seriousness. Musil here stops his playfulness and comes as close to Broch's essayistic approach as he ever probably could come. As ever, context is

all-important. In the preceding chapter, Ulrich visits Clarisse
and her husband, Walter—that other dullard who is the man
with qualities. Clarisse talks to Ulrich about what the proposed Austrian year of the Collateral Campaign should be: a
Nietzsche year, or an Ulrich year. They both speak around the
subject of love, love for each other, undeclared and possibly
unrecognized. Clarisse tells Ulrich, to his astonishment, that
she has urged Walter to kill him. Ulrich says that it is all right
to think such things, but Clarisse responds that action should
follow thought. She herself might kill Ulrich. One must not
let things happen; one must act. Ulrich looms in Clarisse's
mind as the devil; she remarks to Ulrich that at the beginning of their conversation she had only remembered Walter's
begging for a child, the child that she refuses to conceive.
Ulrich begins to explain "why one cannot do anything" anyway, but he cannot or will not go on. Clarisse tries in vain
to hurt him and calls him a "great big criminal." The chapter
ends when they are "disagreeably interrupted" by Walter's
return (II, 62–65). Chapter 82 seems weird if one has not
before met Musil's technique for setting forth the feelings and
actions of women in love. Clarisse is close cousin to many of
Musil's enchanting woman characters: Claudine ("Die Vo-
lendung der Liebe" ("The Perfection of a Love") and Veronica ("Die Versuchung der stillen Veronika" ("The Temptation of Quiet Veronica") foremost, heroines of short fiction
published in 1911. However disturbing, and Musil's women
are always so, the chapter sets the scene for the crucial matter
to follow.

  Chapter 83, entitled "Seinesgleichen geschieht oder
warum erfindet man nicht Geschichte?" ("The like of it
happens, or, Why does one not invent history?") begins thus:

  What could Ulrich have said to Clarisse, anyway?
  He had kept silence because she had aroused in him a queer

desire to utter the word "God." What he had wanted to say was something like this: "God is far from meaning the world literally. The world is an image, an analogy, a figure of speech, that He must make use of for some reason or other, and it is of course always inadequate. We must not take Him at His word; we ourselves must work out the sum that He sets us."

.   .   .   .

But there was something else that he had also had on the tip of his tongue, something about mathematical problems that did not admit of particular solutions, the combining of which brought one nearer to the general solution. He might have added that he regarded the problem set by every human life as one of these. [II, 65.]

Riding the tram on his way home, Ulrich reflects on the notions of flux, complexity, and the multiplicity of events. His thoughts move closer to history through events:

Was there really a war going on in the Balkans, or not? Some sort of intervention was undoubtedly going on, but whether that was war or not he did not exactly know. There were so many things stirring humanity. The record for high-altitude flying had again been broken— . . . A Negro boxer had beaten the white champion, so winning the world championship; Johnson his name was. The President of France had gone to Russia; there was talk of world peace being in danger. [II, 67.]

Ulrich thinks of a tenor making great amounts of money in South America, of an earthquake in Japan.

These were stirring times, round about the end of 1913 and the beginning of 1914. But two years, or five years, earlier the times had also been stirring times: every day had its excitements. And yet one had only a faint memory, or no memory at all, of what had actually been happening then. [II, 67–68.]

History was a peculiar affair indeed, Ulrich thinks (although here Ulrich is transparently Musil). One event or another by now had found its appropriate place in history, or would do so, but whether the event had indeed occurred was not certain. Musil caps the meditation with a passage of his magnificent gibberish:

For what is essential to the occurrence of anything is that it should occur in a particular year and not in another or perhaps not at all; and it is also essential that the occurrence should itself occur, and not merely something similar or the like of it. But that is precisely what nobody can assert of history, unless he happens to have written it down at the same time, as the newspapers do, or unless it is a matter of professional or pecuniary affairs, for it is naturally important to know in how many years one will be entitled to a pension or when one will possess a certain sum of money or have spent it; and in such a context even wars can become memorable affairs. This history of ours looks pretty unsafe and messy, when looked at from close at hand, something like a half-solidified swamp, and then in the end, strangely enough, it turns out there is after all a track running across it, that very "road of history" of which nobody knows whence it comes. [II, 68.]

Ulrich, riding the tram, becomes indignant at the thought that he is *being the material of history.* He is sitting in a machine in motion in process of being made into "something called 'the future'." He leaves the tram at the next stop and continues on foot. He reflects on Clarisse's wanting to declare a Year of the Mind; it is senseless, like Diotima's Collateral Campaign, but why? His first answer is that world history came into existence just as other stories did. Authors never invented anything new, and one author copies another. His second answer is that

history . . . came into existence for the most part without any authors. It evolved not from a centre, but from the periphery, from minor causes. It probably did not take as much as one was given to thinking it did to turn Gothic man or the ancient Greek into modern civilised man. For human nature was equally capable of cannibalism and of the *Critique of Pure Reason*. [II, 69.]

Ulrich then finds disgression one: from his cavalry service, he recalls riding in double file to practice "Passing on orders." The Commander gives an order in a low voice, with instructions that it be passed from man to man. If the order given was "Sergeant-Major move to the head of the column," what emerged at the rear was something like "Eight troopers to be shot immediately." Thus it was that world history came about.

Next, Ulrich's third answer:

if one were therefore to transplant a whole generation of present-day Europeans, while still in their infancy, into the Egypt of the year five thousand B.C. and leave them there, world history would begin all over again at the year five thousand, at first repeating itself for a while and then, for reasons that no man can guess, gradually beginning to deviate.

Digression number two: the law of world history, it now occurred to him, was nothing but the fundamental principle of government in old Kakania, namely that of "muddling through." Kakania was an immensely shrewd State. [II, 69–70.]

Ulrich meets his friend Fischel on the street, and they take up the question together. Ulrich says that he has admitted from the outset that something is very improper about his question,

why does man not make history? That is, why does he only attack history like an animal, when he is hurt, when things are on fire close behind him? Why, in short, does he make history only in an emergency? [II, 71.]

Ulrich ends the dialogue with the thought that

the times of heroical-political history, which was made by hazard
and its knights, were to a large extent obsolete and must be replaced
by a planned answer to the problems, an answer in which all those
whom it concerned would play their part. [II, 71.]

I dwell at such length on Musil's historical chapter because it is central to what I interpret to be his entire purpose
in the novel. He prepares for Ulrich's musings about history
by giving us the disturbing exchange between Ulrich and Clarisse, that Clarisse who is incipiently mad, who threatens
murder, more seriously than not, when she is thwarted, and
who disguises her frustration both to herself, to her husband
Walter, and to Ulrich, in intellectual terms. She admires
Ulrich, despises Walter, wants a child, but not Walter's child.
At the same time, she is a Nietzschean woman, outside or
beyond society, beyond good and evil. Next, Musil gently
picks Hegel up and brushes him off, having earlier put him
down. Ulrich's effort is to set aside the rational in a rational
manner. His orderly teasing of history is at once a negation of
Clarisse's Nietzschean streak and an ironic affirmation of
Hegel's theory of the will in history. Nevertheless, the role
of the will, what Ulrich thinks of as "the times of heroical-
political history," are obsolete.

Ulrich, and Musil, has on one level of meaning and
intention cleared the decks for Agathe, Ulrich's mysterious
sister, who will transcendently symbolize the possibility of
human love in all its manifestations; intellectual space has
been made for Musil's adventure into the suprarational, into
the mystical, in fact. Through his irony, we may discover
Musil's denial of skepticism, and his search through philosophy of history for a method that will satisfactorily account for
the past and leave open the future.

Less obvious even in lengthy quotation is the fact that

all this matter is saved from sailing off into the empyrean, of leaving the genre of the novel (in the manner of Broch in his third volume), by Musil's subtle and prophetic parallel to the shape of European history, specifically of German history to come. Moosbrugger's madness, Clarisse's emotional excesses, Meingast's prophecies, even General Stumm von Bordwehr's doublethink and doubletalk — all take on resonance from Musil's foreknowledge of the Thousand Year Reich to follow. Musil's title to the third volume of the novel, published in his lifetime, *Ins Tausendjährige Reich (Die Verbrecher)*, is to the point. The Kaisers translate that title as *Into the Millennium,* so avoiding the Hitlerian overtone, but also avoiding the resonance that Musil's original must have to anyone with the German language in his ear and German history in his memory.

Apart from the fact that Musil's novel does not end, and that any shape it has is the shape of the author's life, and that by definition most of our lives are shapeless, we encounter in the vast sprawl of the latter half of the manuscripts, and indeed in Musil's third volume, too, an apparent shift in tone and direction, although the matter of arrangement one again notes is subject to controversy. It seems to me that as the decade of the 1930's went on, Musil turned away from history, from events, that all too clearly impinged upon every writer, to his utopian vision.[9] We can see a rough parallel in his notebooks and correspondence: a shift in mood, a change in viewpoint which emerges in points of emphasis rather than in dramatic statement.

Controversy apart, Musil's millennial or utopian material is of great pertinence to my thesis concerning the nature of post-Romanticism. First, the nature of the shift in mood or density is indicated through incident. Ulrich's father dies. Ulrich travels to the provincial town where his father lived in order to settle the estate, and there he meets his sister, Agathe, virtually unknown to him (and completely unknown to us). Agathe describes Ulrich as her twin; [10] she has been divorced; she is attractive; she unscrupulously intends to alter their father's will in order to clarify an annoying clause. Promptly, surprisingly for the reader, Ulrich knows that he loves her. Again Musil defies paraphrase:

Now it suddenly struck him that not only had Agathe somehow got from him what she had said about truth, but what she was doing in the other room [altering their father's will] was also something he had outlined. It was after all he who had said that in the highest state a human being could reach there was no longer any such thing as Good and Evil, only faith or doubt; that definite rules were contrary to the essential nature of morality, and that faith must never be more than at the most an hour old; that when acting in a state of faith one could not do anything beastly; and that intuition was a more passionate state than truth. And now here was Agathe on the point of leaving the confines of the moral territory, about to venture out upon those limitless deeps where there is no other criterion than whether a thing will lift one up or let one down. She was carrying it out in the same way as, that other time, she had taken the decorations out of his hesitant hand, in order to exchange them. And at this moment, regardless of her lack of conscience, he loved her, with the strange feeling that it was his own thoughts that had gone from him to her and were now returning from her to him, now poorer in reasoning but, like a creature of the wild, with an elusive odour of freedom about them. [III, 154–155.]

The thought occurs to them that they should live together, Ulrich and Agathe, and we have this exchange, prophetic of much matter to follow:

"We'll live like hermits," Agathe had said with a gay smile. "But as for love-affairs, of course each of us will be free. At any rate there's no impediment in your way!" she assured him.

"Do you realise," Ulrich said by way of answer, "that we shall be entering into the Millennium?"

"What does that mean?"

"We've talked so much about the sort of love that has no goal, that isn't like a flowing stream, but like the sea—a state of existence! Now tell me honestly: When they told you at school that the angels in Paradise did nothing but behold the countenance of the Lord and glorify Him, were you able to imagine that bliss of doing nothing and thinking nothing?"

"I always thought it must be a bit boring—though I'm sure I've only my own imperfection to blame," Agathe had replied.

"But bearing in mind all we've agreed about," Ulrich declared, "imagine that sea as a state of immobility and detachment filled to the brim with everlasting crystal-clear eventfulness. In past ages people have tried to imagine such a life upon earth: that's the Millennium, the Kingdom of a Thousand Years, formed in our own image and yet not among any of the kingdoms that we know. Well, that's the way we'll live! We shall cast off all egoism, we shall not accumulate possessions or knowledge or lovers or friends or principles, not even ourselves. Accordingly our spirit will open up, becoming fluid in relation to man and beast, opening out till we're no longer ourselves and maintain ourselves solely by being interwoven with the whole world!" [III, 159.]

We have left the world of Evelyn Waugh (Musil has been compared to Waugh in the force of his satire),[11] and we have left the reality of the social world to move closer to the atmosphere of *Cymbeline* or *The Winter's Tale*. That is to say that there is something of Shakespeare's late and often puzzling comedies about Musil's intellectual utopia. Musil's many discussions with himself in the notebooks indicate that he knew the risks he was taking in trying to make definite, to make into a novel of manners material that he could not give form to except, perhaps, by way of mathematical formulas. "Scharf denken kann mann immer" ("one can always think acutely"), he warned himself. It is in his awareness of the necessity for intellectual precision even in the midst of the most Romantic quest that he takes his place among the post-Romantics. He is the novelist of the pluperfect conditional: "If in earlier days Diotima had been wakened from her sleep and asked what she wanted, she would have answered, without having to stop and think, that the power of love in a living soul yearned to communicate itself to the whole world . . ." (II, 32–33). This is *scharf denken* indeed, a delightfully realized ability to make lucid the soggy heavings and bubblings of a dim mind, in this instance, Diotima's. Or that of General Stumm von Bordwehr, all five feet four of whom are sexually attracted to the statuesque Diotima, but who knows that she is out of his reach: his arms could not encompass Diotima, for they are "intellectually short." Musil's post-Romanticism is in the figure of Ulrich, who as ironic hero, as intellectual hero, is still in the pure or historical Romantic manner, heroic. He is heroic in his lucidity: he thinks of Diotima:

The Mind of this woman, who would have been so beautiful without her mind, aroused an inhuman feeling in him, perhaps a fear of the mind, a distaste for all great things, a feeling that was quite faint, scarcely detectable — and perhaps even the word "feeling" was far too pretentious an expression for something that was but a mere breath. [I, 341.]

And Romanticism accounts for Ulrich's principle in which we may hear a distant but clear echo of the first German generation of Romantics: "reality has in itself a nonsensical yearning for unreality" (I, 343). The distinction in Ulrich's thought between the historically Romantic and post-Romantic lies only in the word "unsinnig" ("nonsensical").

Ulrich's view of Good and Evil provides a textbook application of Morse Peckham's definition of negative Romanticism, that state in which one order of mind and nature has been lost, and a reordering not yet found.[12] Ulrich reflects that

The mind has learned that beauty can make things good, bad, stupid or enchanting. The mind dissects and analyses a sheep and a penitent sinner and finds humility and patience in both. It investigates a substance and observes that in large quantities it is a poison, in smaller quantities a stimulant. It knows that the mucous membrane of the lips is related to the mucous membrane of the intestine, but knows too that the humility of those lips is related to the humility of all that is saintly. It mixes things up, unravels them again and forms new combinations. Good and evil, above and below, are for it not relative ideas tinged with scepticism, but terms of a function, values dependent on the context in which they appear. It has learnt from the centuries that vices may turn into virtues and virtues into vices, and actually regards it as sheer clumsiness if one does not in one lifetime succeed in turning a criminal into a useful citizen. It does not recognise anything as in itself permissible or impermissible, for anything may have a quality by which it some day becomes part of a great new relationship. It secretly has a mortal hatred of everything that behaves as though it were established once and for all, the great ideals and laws and their little fossilised imprint, the hedged-in character. It regards nothing as firmly established, neither any personality nor any order of things or ideas. Because our knowledge may change with every day, it believes in no ties, and everything possesses the value that it has only until the next act of creation, as a face to which one is speaking changes even while the words are being spoken. [I, 178–179.]

Here and in succeeding episodes we have Lord Byron in twentieth-century guise, wit, irony, and all, not excluding incest. Musil's use of the theme of incest, first hinted at in Ulrich's attraction to his cousin, Diotima, next in Clarisse's story of her father's attempt upon her, and most fully developed in the Ulrich-Agathe relationship, derives from an impulse similar to Byron's. For the Romantic, incest is the fullest expression of ego, a form of self-love. Although we may find a rationalization for incest in Ulrich's thoughts about Good and Evil above, Musil's use of incest is less a parallel to Byronic egotism and eroticism than it is evidence of Musil's

post-Romantic fascination with the chameleon-like change-
ableness of historical reality, his doubts about various philos-
ophies of history, and his search, through the single, inces-
tuous Ulrich-Agathe figure—and they are one, not two—for a
satisfactory philosophy of history and of nature.

Musil and Broch overlap in their common use of the idea
of redemption, of the possibility of a Messiah. Broch concludes *Die Schlafwandler* on that note, and Musil thought of
calling his novel *Der Erlöser* (The Redeemer). But in *Der
Mann ohne Eigenschaften* as we now know it, redemption
is presented first satirically through the person of General
Stumm von Bordwehr. The General has connived his way
uninvited to the meetings of the Collateral Campaign committee, urged on by his awareness that something is afoot,
and where something is afoot, the army should of course be
involved. He is confused by Arnheim and the rest of the
"people of intellect" whom he encounters, reflecting at one
point that he himself was thinking too much. He is fed up
with the intellectuals:

Their thoughts were never at peace, beholding that eternally wandering element, the final, undefined factor in all things, which never
finds its proper place anywhere. And so they finally became convinced that the age in which they were living was fated to be one of
spiritual barrenness and could only be redeemed from that condition by some remarkable happening or some quite remarkable person. This was how, among what were called intellectual people,
there at that time arose the popularity of the semantic complex
"redemption." There was a conviction that everything would come
to a standstill if some Messiah did not come soon. This was, as the
case might be, a medical Messiah, who would redeem the healing
art from the academic researches that went on while people fell ill
and died without getting help or, say, a poetic Messiah capable of
writing a drama that would sweep millions of people into the

theatres and yet at the same time be utterly original and unique in
its spiritual sublimity. And apart from this conviction that every
single human activity could in fact only be restored to its proper
condition through the agency of a special Messiah, there was of
course also the simple and in every respect wholesome desire for a
strong-armed Messiah to deal with the situation as a whole. So that
age just before the Great War was a rather Messianic age, and if
even whole nations wanted to be redeemed, that did not really
amount to anything special and unusual. [II, 267.]

   Musil's reflections on the Messiah are not so much a
vision of as an allusion to history which, like his other allusions to history, combine to the erection of a structure, open-
sided and incomplete, that in turn reveals even on its unfinished surfaces another order of vision, utopian and mystical.
Theology apart, the term "mystical" is always unsatisfactory,
for it suggests evasion on the part of the user. Many commentators have preferred psychological explanations for
Musil's dilemma, his apparent inability to reconcile social,
political, and historical material with his intuition of possible
salvation for humanity. In the psychologizers' minds lies the
fact that Musil had undergone treatment by an Adlerian
analyst in the late 1920's.[13] Musil's deep seriousness even in
his most antic moments, however, his concern that aesthetics
serve ethics, together with his extraordinary degree of intellectual and stylistic control, do not yield to mere psychological solutions; nor should they. Musil's work is psychological in the sense that all fiction is psychological in a certain
measure; it is not psychoanalytical, however. Musil's early
work anticipates psychoanalysis. *Der Mann ohne Eigenschaften*, even when concerned with the motifs of psychoanalysis:
sexuality, identity, the nature of the ego, is delightfully free
of psychoanalytical formulas and cliché. Ulrich-Agathe's
vision of happiness, of ecstasy indeed, is mystical, then, in

the sense that it approaches a religious rather than a psychological dimension.

Broch's final vision is distinctly visionary, and rather
closer to history than is Musil's. The conclusion of *Huguenau
oder die Sachlichkeit,* and therefore of the entire trilogy,
begins with Broch's characteristic lyrical essay in which the
insistent voice of the narrator-author ranges through history
to expound upon the terrifying prospect of Huguenau, that
Huguenau who survives the war by deserting his unit, who
rapes, murders, and robs his way into the postwar middle
class. In the passage in question, Huguenau is seen as a kind
of moral Ahasuerus, wandering through space and time, and
the society that made him possible as lost, uprooted, unrooted,
without standards, outcast too. Broch's meaning more than
previously in the trilogy lies in the diction and rhythm of his
prose:

Great is the anguish of the man who becomes aware of his isolation and seeks to escape from his own memory; he is obsessed and
outcast, flung back into the deepest animal anguish, into the anguish
of the creature that suffers violence and inflicts violence, flung back
into an overwhelming loneliness in which his flight and his despair and his stupor may become so great that he cannot help thinking
of inflicting violence on himself so as to escape the immutable law
of events. And in his fear of the voice of judgment that threatens to
issue from the darkness, there awakens within him a doubly strong
yearning for a Leader to take him tenderly and lightly by the hand, to
set things in order and show him the way; a Leader who is nobody's
follower and who will precede him on the untrodden path of the
closed circle and lead him on to ever-higher reaches, to an ever-
brighter revelation; the Leader who will build the house anew that
the dead may come to life again, and who himself has risen again
from the multitude of the dead; the Healer who by his own actions
will give a meaning to the incomprehensible events of the age, so
that Time can begin anew. That is his yearning. Yet even if the

Leader were to come the hoped-for miracle would not happen. . . .
[P. 647.]

Broch goes on at length about that life: stricken and difficult
as all men's lives must be. Then the trilogy concludes on this
note:

> And despite all that: the mere hope of wisdom from a Leader is
> wisdom for us, the mere divination of grace is grace, and unavail-
> ing as may be our hope that in a Leader's visible life the Absolute
> will one day fulfil itself on earth, yet our goal remains accessible,
> our hope that a Messiah will lead us to it remains imperishable, and
> the renascence of values is fated to recur. And hemmed in as we may
> be by the increasing muteness of the abstract, each man a victim of
> the iciest necessity, flung into nothingness, his ego flung to the
> winds — it is the breath of the Absolute that sweeps across the world,
> and from our dim inklings and gropings for truth there will spring
> up the high-day and holiday assurance with which we shall know
> that every man has the divine spark in his soul and that our oneness
> cannot be forfeited; unforfeitable the brotherhood of humble human
> creatures, from whose deepest anguish there shines unforfeitable
> and unforfeited the anguish of a divine grace, the oneness of all
> men, gleaming in all things, beyond all Space and all Time; the
> oneness in which all light has its source and from which springs the
> healing of all living things — symbol of a symbol, image of an image,
> emerging from the destiny that is sinking in darkness, welling up
> out of madness and dreamlessness like the gift of maternal life
> wrested from the unknown and rewon as a heritage, the prototype
> of all imagery rising in the insurrection of the irrational, blotting out
> the self and transcending its confines, annulling time and distance;
> in the icy hurricane, in the tempest of collapse all the doors spring
> open, the foundations of our prison are troubled, and from the pro-
> foundest darkness of the world, from our bitterest and profoundest
> darkness the cry of succour comes to the helpless, there sounds the
> voice that binds all that has been to all that is to come, that binds our
> loneliness to all other lonelinesses, and it is not the voice of dread
> and doom; it falters in the silence of the Logos and yet is borne on
> by it, raised high over the clamour of the non-existent; it is the voice

of man and of the tribes of men, the voice of comfort and hope and immediate love: "Do thyself no harm! for we are all here!" [P. 648.]

In this curious effusion, two contradictory processes are at work simultaneously: a prophetic and despairing anticipation of the historical Führer who came to the apocalyptic rescue of the Huguenaus and of the nation at large; second, an illogical, lyrical invocation of an historical solution that denies the very ground Broch has covered. It is characteristic of one kind of Romanticism to lapse into the lyrical whenever an impossible statement, vision, or intuition has to be conveyed. Broch was willingly Romantic in his final statement. Musil, sharing the same historical basis for his disposition to the mystical-utopian, refused the lyrical impulse, even though his realized, novelistic material led him inexorably to Broch's mystical, quasi-religious conclusion. There, too, may lie still another reason for Musil's inability to conclude his work: his intelligent perception that his final paragraph might read like Hermann Broch's. Both men's vision was finally defeated by history; both gave us intimations of myth, and myth, as Collingwood said, is not at all concerned with human actions.[14] Whatever the novel may be, it does seem to be concerned with the human.

CHAPTER 4

William Faulkner, the Past, and History

Although William Faulkner (1897–1962) was a younger contemporary, the contrast between him, on the one hand, and Robert Musil (1880–1942) and Hermann Broch (1886–1951), on the other, is dramatic, and at first glance, irreconcilable. Whatever their differences, the two Austrian writers have taken their places (belatedly to be sure) [1] in the first rank of distinctively European writers; and by European, we usually have in mind that continental writer of high and dedicated seriousness, intellectual, schooled in the literary and philosophical traditions of the West. Faulkner, like some other American writers, has seemed to many readers to be self-invented, idiosyncratic, isolated from the main stream of Western culture, unschooled and impenetrable. That such an impression is false does not need to be argued. Faulkner's own public front accounted in part for the inaccuracy. That Faulkner is close to Musil and Broch in historical sensibility does need to be argued. It is not merely whimsical, indeed, to see Faulkner's historical sensibility as deriving, however indirectly, from early Romanticism, specifically from Novalis: let the argument begin there.

In my first chapter, I quoted with reference to Faulkner from Novalis' *Fragmente* the statement that "We bear the burdens of our fathers . . . , and we actually live in the past and the future and are nowhere less at home than in the present." I noted that Novalis' statement was useful for establishing one kind of relationship to history which is present both in Proust's work and in Faulkner's. Now I shall try to refine that generalization with reference to Faulkner, and take for an additional text still another of Novalis' *Fragmente:* "The historian must often turn orator. For he intones the gospels; all history is nothing but a gospel" [2] This is pertinent not for its view of history as gospel, a view that is simply wrong, but for Novalis' brilliant perception of connection between history and a certain style of mind and of prose. Novalis helps one to define a central quality of Faulkner's style, the oratorical; to do so in an orderly manner, however, one must again go to Romanticism to supply a term missing from the large body of criticism that by now threatens to overwhelm Faulkner's primary work, his prose fiction.

It may not be completely obvious that American Romanticism and American post-Romanticism are not identical with their European prototypes, and that one cannot take it for granted that one can discuss Faulkner or any other American in the same context as that for Proust, Broch, or Musil. Just as the American landscape of the year 1800 differed from the European landscape, so American society differed from European; and, of at least equal significance, the American language increasingly differed from the English. The American intellectual tradition, on the other hand, differed less from the European than did the language. Where considerable differences occur, they result from matters of emphasis

and time. By time, one means the lag between the appearance of a document, a book, or a fashion on one continent and
the other. Because of the unfixed quality of American society,
European movements looked different in America owing to
the very tenacity and self-consciousness of the relatively few
Americans who indulged in the life of the mind, whether as
artists, philosophers, or however. In terms of language, we
have Harold Rosenberg's vigorous testimony: "Whoever
speaks the American language is forced into romanticism. His
strictest discipline is itself a spiritual oddity, and gives birth
to an oddity—as witness *The Scarlet Letter*, Emily Dickinson,
the early gas engine. The American landscape is not easily
mistaken for an endless wallpaper of nymphs and fountains—in this language it takes hard application to achieve
academic deadness." [3] Where Broch and Musil regarded
Romanticism in terms derived from Kant, Hegel, and Nietzsche, as a movement decidedly historical and to be used for
ironic effect when used consciously, the American, Faulkner,
came to his essentially Romantic task in quite different terms.

   For Faulkner, born in 1897, Romanticism was not historical, not a movement of the preceding half-century and
deeper in time, but to the contrary an integral part and context of everyday life in his native Mississippi. He did not read
Kant, like Broch, nor Nietzsche, like Musil. He liked to pre-
tend that he read nothing at all except the labels on whiskey
bottles, a pretense to primitivism that, in the American mode,
was itself part of his Romanticism. Whatever Faulkner did or
did not read, we may readily see in his published work that
his Romanticism came to him not by way of Schelling, but
by way of Emerson and the Concord School. One strain in
American Romanticism, the dominant one, was distinctly
transcendental. It combined sharpness of observation, precision in diction, and the most evanescent faith in a mystical

principle of unity with some manner of godhead—the Oversoul in Emerson's system—such unity to be attained through disciplined perception of the self in relation to physical Nature (capitalized). The American Romantic tradition, for one of Faulkner's generation, or for that matter, our own, was not remote in time. It was alive and tangible, whether in the schoolroom or in the rhetoric of politicians' speeches, not excluding politicians in Mississippi. It is apparent in Faulkner's extraordinary apprehension of nature in all his best work, but most vividly in "The Bear," and in his mastery of diction. His early leaning to traditional European Romanticism, on the other hand, is painfully present in the Keatsian pastiches of *The Marble Faun* (verse, 1924).

Another quality in American life that is if anything exaggerated in Faulkner's work, a quality directly related to Romanticism, is awareness of history. That awareness is so intense, so cultivated throughout American society, so self-conscious as to appear, to the European, as a kind of national neurosis. By and large, the European takes history for granted, history as opposed to nationality. The American sees history in terms of biography and in terms of event; his is a naïve view that results in the establishment of Freedom Trails, Blue-Star Freeways, elaborate notices in wheat fields to commemorate Indian skirmishes, and bronze plates on every wall, bush, and fence. For Faulkner, history is the Civil War, the War Between the States. That war is forever the centerpiece, its antecedents and results secondary but still absorbing. Virtually every major character whom Faulkner created says or implies, "The past isn't dead. It ain't even past." The statement could stand as epigraph to Faulkner's entire output.

A third quality of Faulkner and of American post-Romanticism, equal only to Faulkner's obsession with history, is his self-consciousness about writing, about being or not being an

artist. The exigencies of American frontier life and the per-
petuation in many reaches of society of the frontier outlook
on life and letters combined to discourage imaginative work.
That attitude helped to cut off American artists from one
another, while it forced a self-consciousness that produced,
for one effect, the illusion in the American writer that no one
before him had ever written a book. That in turn contributed
to a possibly exaggerated esteem for the notion of experiment
and to the illusion that in fact, not only in fancy, each writer
was the first upon the unsullied field of his art. The modern
prominence of the idea of experimentation in art may be seen
as a form of Romantic optimism, an overwhelming faith in the
self, and in the nearly religious power of art. History, experiment, obsession, compulsion, isolation: one has seen them
before in other forms and as the products of minds more conventionally disciplined than Faulkner's. It is time to see the
shape of those characteristics in some of Faulkner's work.

Few novelists' work varies in quality so widely as does
Faulkner's. Here I want only to concentrate on Faulkner
at his finest, as in *The Sound and the Fury* (1929) and *Light
in August* (1932), and to mark how brief and intense his
apprenticeship was by allusion to his first two novels, *Soldier's Pay* (1926) and *Mosquitoes* (1927). Set in Georgia and
New Orleans respectively, those first novels are garrulous and
unfocused. Faulkner's tone is uncertain in *Soldier's Pay;*
his account of the wounded Donald Mahon's return after the
war to his native Georgia seems to challenge in turn Sopho-
cles, Shakespeare, and George Ade. *Mosquitoes* is adjectival,
formless, and uncontrolled. In his first two novels, Faulkner
had found neither his locale nor his own voice. He wrote
in pastiche of T. S. Eliot and Sherwood Anderson, by turns.
Faulkner made almost all his mistakes, however, in those
first two novels. His later mediocrity in *The Town* (1957),

The Mansion (1959), and *The Reivers* (1962) is the product of self-parody and diminution of energy, quite another order of difficulty.

By the time of *Sartoris* (1929), Faulkner not only had found his region, Yoknapatawpha County, Mississippi, and most of the themes that would occupy him for the next thirty years but he had also reached the border of the prose style and the narrative techniques that would remain peculiarly his own. *Sartoris* is transitional, although the transition was swift and much of it had been accomplished in the writing of that novel. Faulkner found his enduring subject in his own region, northern Mississippi, and in his own family. Colonel Sartoris is modeled in part upon Faulkner's great-grandfather, Colonel Falkner (as the original spelling was). In recovering his own family's past, however, Faulkner was not merely resorting to history as past event; rather, in *Sartoris* and more fully in succeeding novels, he was gradually uncovering a philosophy of time, and simultaneously, in a characteristically American manner, working out an idea about the American relationship to history. The two themes, time and historical apprehension, are intertwined to a degree that Europeans have difficulty in sorting them out.

That difficulty is most obvious in the two novels of Faulkner that Europeans admire inordinately: *Sanctuary* (1931), and *Pylon* (1935). Albert Camus, for example, wrote that those two novels are masterpieces; [4] they are two novels that American criticism, in the main, finds inferior. André Malraux, who recognized Faulkner before anyone else, European or American, wrote in his preface to the French translation of *Sanctuary* that it "is the intrusion of Greek tragedy into the detective story." [5] Jean-Paul Sartre, in an essay of 1947, "Time in Faulkner: *The Sound and the Fury*," decided that Faulkner's metaphysics are faulty because, through his manipulations of time, no provision for a future is possible. All is historical, all in the past. Quentin Compson's suicide itself is past when, through Faulkner as manipulator, Quentin relives the last day of his life.

Sartre further notes that we have already been where Faulkner takes us: in Proust. The confusions of chronology as opposed to their mechanical order, the emotional arrangement of events in Quentin's mind, are the order of Proust's mind as well. But the significant difference between Proust and Faulkner, for Sartre, is that where Proust discovers salvation in time itself, in the recovery of time past, for Faulkner the past is never lost, however much, like a mystic, he may want to forget or ignore time. Both Proust and Faulkner emphasize the transitoriness of emotion, of the condition of love or misery or whatever passes because it is transitory in time. According to Sartre, Proust really *should have* used a technique like Faulkner's, for "that was the logical outcome of his metaphysic. Faulkner, however, is a lost man, and because he knows that he is lost he risks pushing his thought to its conclusion. Proust is a classicist and a Frenchman; and the French lose themselves with caution and always end by finding themselves. Eloquence, a love of clarity and a rational mind led Proust to preserve at least the appearance of chronology." [6]

What strikes the American reader in Malraux's and Camus's statements is that they single out for special comment *Sanctuary*, and *Pylon*, the two novels written after Faulkner's apprenticeship that are not concerned with history, novels that are, accordingly, least characteristic of him, although more readily available to the European mind, perhaps, than *Sartoris* or *The Sound and the Fury*. Sartre, on the other hand, sees what an American would call history solely in terms of metaphysics and a Proustian conception of time. Of necessity the element of time is prominent in Faulkner, for one can neither perceive nor write historically without becoming involved in considerations of time. One sees here, I think, the informing difference between the European post-Hegelian (Sartre) and the American post-Emersonian (Faulkner). For the European, the order of march is time, then history. For the American, history precedes time.

The European perceives history as a philosophical problem and addresses it in metaphysical language. The American, closer than the European to Romantic origins, sees history in terms of perception, consciousness, and apprehension of self. With the exception of Henry Adams, Americans do not think or write philosophically about history. The European, by contrast, is at his ease with history. He can take it or leave it as circumstance warrants. When he confronts history, he becomes a Vico, a Hegel, a Carlyle, a Dilthey, an Aron. When the American confronts history, he has the conviction that he is confronting himself, which is to say that he treats history through art rather than through philosophy. History for him is recent and urgent. Just beyond the tall buildings is the illusion of wilderness. Just back there in the family album are images of pioneers or immigrants, and no distinction need be made, for both pioneers and immigrants were people who began existence anew with the illusion of rebirth. History leans heavily on the American, and when he becomes uncomfortable, he says *Good-Bye, Wisconsin,* like Glenway Wescott; or like Faulkner, he writes of fourteen-year-old boys in the American South like Charles Mallison, "who had wanted of course to leave his mark too on his time," who feel condemned to anonymity because they were not born in time to fight in a War Between the States or

any other heroic encounter offered their forefathers. Faulkner by way of young Mallison's uncle, Gavin Stevens, offers
comfort:

"It's all *now* you see. Yesterday wont be over until tomorrow and
tomorrow began ten thousand years ago. For every Southern boy
fourteen years old, not once but whenever he wants it, there is the
instant when it's still not yet two o'clock on that July afternoon
in 1863, the brigades are in position behind the rail fence, the guns
are laid and ready in the woods and the furled flags are already
loosened to break out and Pickett himself with his long oiled ringlets and his hat in one hand probably and his sword in the other
looking up the hill waiting for Longstreet to give the word and it's
all in the balance, it hasn't happened yet, it hasn't even begun yet,
it not only hasn't begun yet but there is still time for it not to begin
against that position and those circumstances which made more men
than Garnett and Kemper and Armstead and Wilcox look grave yet
it's going to begin, we all know that, we have come too far with too
much at stake and that moment doesn't need even a fourteen-year-
old boy to think *This time. Maybe this time* with all this much to
lose and all this much to gain: Pennsylvania, Maryland, the world,
the golden dome of Washington itself to crown with desperate and
unbelievable victory the desperate gamble, the cast made two years
ago; or to anyone who ever sailed even a skiff under a quilt sail, the
moment in 1492 when somebody thought *This is it:* the absolute
edge of no return, to turn back now and make home or sail irrevocably on and either find land or plunge over the world's roaring
rim. . . ." [7]

Intruder in the Dust, of 1948, from which this is quoted
is not vintage Faulkner, but because Faulkner had covered
the ground so often, he was able to place in a congested paragraph the theme of complete, earlier novels. Faulkner's prose
might be compared to the work of a composer at the piano who
looks for the right combination of notes and tempo to set him
off with authority. Here it is history, the historical vision, that
gives Faulkner his authority. Gavin Stevens' vision is not

positivistic history, but a Romantic vision which may perform the function of objective history if one is not fussy about facts, or if one is more interested in using history than in philosophizing about it. American criticism needed more than twenty years to determine that Faulkner was not an apologist for southern racism, a writer obsessed with madness, violence, and lurid crime, but one whose vision was encompassing, compassionate, and universal. As early as 1931, it might have been clear that Faulkner was not a novelist of fragmentary and hysterical moments of intensity, but one who wrote large on a historical canvas. Hints of a large frame were present in *Sartoris* (1929), but by the time of *The Sound and the Fury* and the short stories of *These Thirteen* (1930–1931), Faulkner had given ample evidence of what he was about.

In contrast to his first two novels, *The Sound and the Fury* demonstrated experiment as mastery, experiment that justified Faulkner's heavy demands upon his readers. At the same time, that novel indicated fully the angles and depth of Faulkner's historical vision. In form a *Ring and the Book* telling and retelling of Candace Compson's loss of virginity, her subsequent pregnancy and marriage, the novel in fact is a history of the Compson family, of the South, of black-white relationships, a social satire, and a haunting meditation upon time and human destiny. Faulkner's awareness of history is implicit on every page, in every character, and in every formal device. By beginning the circular narration in the mind of Benjy Compson, the thirty-three-year-old idiot, Faulkner achieves the high degree of intensity necessary to his second narration, that of Quentin on the final day of his life. Faulkner also constructs a symbolic reading of southern history through his "mad" retelling of a mad family's destruction.

Benjy as a symbol of dissolution provides an example of successful use of a technique that rarely convinces in modern

fiction, witness Faulkner's own unfortunate *A Fable* (1954), or
Hemingway's *The Old Man and the Sea*. In every sense, Benjy
is natural, and exactly right. Without his love for Candace
(Caddy), without his sense of her loss, we could not accept
Quentin's passionate attachment to Caddy, nor his resulting
suicide by drowning in the Charles River. Quentin is the
Compson family's last hope, the Compsons who have produced in their time Governors and Generals, Confederate of
course; whose wealth has been squandered by folly and
drink, whose square mile of land has been reduced almost to
nothing, the final sale being that of Benjy's pasture to pay for
one year at Harvard for Quentin. Quentin is a frail hope, for
his life is dominated by Caddy, and by a Calvinist sense of sin
to such a degree that he confesses to his alcoholic father an
act of incest that he has not committed, in the hope of "saving"
Caddy from her own sexuality. He can no more save her than,
in a crucial passage, he can at her urging cut her throat with
his pocket knife. Although Caddy is the focus of Quentin's
despair, she is only part of a larger and overwhelming sense of
the fate of a culture that kills him.

After the high tragedy of Quentin's death, the low comedy
of Jason's narration of events is necessary and welcome relief.
Jason, every inch his miserable, sniveling mother's boy, is the
Snopes principle at work among the once noble Compsons.
For Faulkner, the Snopeses represent the red-neck, poor
white trash who take over the South from the exhausted first
families. Always happy with a tall tale, Faulkner in the tale
of Jason's self-undoing through thievery from his own mother
and from Caddy, his niece, produces one of the tallest and
most successful. Having read an exalted, Shakespearian narration through Quentin, we welcome Jason's account for
bringing us back to subnormalcy, to the killing, practical outlook that Faulkner associates with money-making, carpet-

baggery, and the Snopes family: all dominant waves in the history of the post-Civil War South. Jason, too, is rendered fictionally but observed historically.

The fourth and final narration is technically Faulkner's, who writes in the third person, but emotionally it belongs to old Dilsey, the Compson family servant who with her own family has served the Compsons throughout their adversity, whose moral judgment is impeccable, and whose humanity attains to greatness. In having suffered the silliness and hypochondria of "Miss Cahline" (the Compson children's mother), in her love for Benjy, for Quentin (Caddy's bastard daughter), in her strength and her humility, Dilsey is a black saint, a memorable tribute to Faulkner's awareness of the foulness of slavery and its meaning for the modern South. Dilsey is further proof that Faulkner is most fully historical when he is most fully fictional. We need only to hear him preaching sermons on political issues, particularly on black-white, North-South attitudes in *Intruder in the Dust* and elsewhere in the later fiction for a textbook example of how history does and does not get into prose fiction.

More than forty years after publication, *The Sound and the Fury* remains as fresh as the day it came off Faulkner's typewriter. It has the early spring freshness of other works which seem tied by theme to their historical period but are not: *Middlemarch*, or *Le Rouge et le noir*, or Svevo's *Zeno*. What creates such apparent immortality in a work of fiction? In the case of *The Sound and the Fury*, it is that the novel has scarcely a flaw, because the form and the meaning are inseparable, because the complexity of narration is appropriate to the intellectual process that makes inevitable the often confusing and ambiguous changes in time, in tone, and in focus. Because without exception the characters are sharp, their dialogue registered with an ease that conceals a high degree of stylization, more real than reality yet imagined and fictional, and because Faulkner is not afraid to love and to hate them. He is not the objective naturalist, and he can take sides yet avoid melodrama. He loves Benjy, Caddy, Dilsey, Quentin, and Jason Compson, senior; he hates young Jason and his whining mother. Careless readers often see Faulkner's girls as identical and even interchangeable, constructed on the lines of the vicious Temple Drake, of *Sanctuary*, and all as examples of his personal hatred for the sex: in Jason's words, "Once a bitch, always a bitch. . . ." Faulkner seemed fascinated by the type of the flapper, but he loved Caddy. Love is reflected in her love for Benjy and Quentin, her brothers; in her respect for her father, and obversely in Caroline Compson's luxuriating in her own disapproval of her daughter's behavior. Faulkner is one of the few writers we have who could create memorable children without cuteness or sentimentality.

These qualities alone, however, fail sufficiently to account for his total achievement; they account only for his position as experimenter. Faulkner's distinction in his best work lies in his uncanny ability to unite two apparently mutually hostile elements: pictorial realism and transcendent symbol, or, dread word, myth. He could bring about that union because of the nature of southern history, and because his energy derived from the southern American inability to leave history to history, to the past; and it derived from Faulkner's perception of how the past pervaded the present, creating for him an apocalyptic, if not tragic prospect.

Unlike Yeats, Eliot, or Hemingway, writers who either invented a mythology of their own or went to cultural anthropology for symbols from which to create a mythology, Faulkner either knew in his conscious mind or knew in his novelist's bones that southern history itself could provide a usable mythology. All he needed to do was to talk to the neighbors and go to his own family records to uncover material for a lifetime of fiction. The legend that Faulkner found in native sources was the familiar one of the unvanquished, of the gentlemen out of Scott who went off to the Civil War to defend a civilized, humane way of life, their oiled ringlets flowing in the wind, only to be beaten, but not vanquished, by a civilization of bastard mechanics and greasy machines. It was a legend of chivalrous sportsmen brought up on the Greek and Latin classics, men too essentially fine to survive the machinations of a lesser, northern breed whose ways were imposed on the South by force of arms. It was a legend of the happy darky, devoted to his master to the point of death, a slave yet free in his protection from the harshness of life, with which in any event he could not cope.

As another southern writer has demonstrated,[8] World War I put an end to the elegiac view that the South held of itself, a view that Faulkner knew to be false, yet one that he honored for the small portion of it that was noble and honorable. The World War hauled the South screaming into the 1920's. Faulkner hated the process, hated the new cities of the "new South," which is why he needed for locale Mississippi, not the Georgia of his first novel, nor the New Orleans of his second, and why he needed to invent the world of Yoknapatawpha County. The "new South" was a product of history as progress. Faulkner's South was a product of a much older conception of history as spiral or circular, a history of repetition in which the past not only illuminates the present, but might very well *be* the present. No European wrote like Faulkner; no European needed to, not even the Germans who in the 1920's shared with the post-Civil War southern Americans the legend of themselves as the unvanquished. Ranke had given the Germans the truth that the past can be scientifically recovered. Faulkner, in producing great fiction, gave us the truth that the truth about the past is as varying as Benjy's (an idiot's), and Quentin's (a suicide's), and Jason's (a petty thief's), and Dilsey's (an illiterate's) views of it. In large part that insight into historical truth accounts for one's judgment that *The Sound and the Fury* not only is Faulkner's finest work but is among the very finest novels of the past century.[9]

Faulkner's treatment of history in *Light in August* (1932) is basically different from that of *The Sound and the Fury*; it at once shows us Faulkner's versatility, and how completely his imagination was charged with his vision of history. The narrative of the birth, suffering, and death of Joe Christmas takes place in the fictional present; it has little to do with Yoknapatawpha County or the Compsons and their family ramifications. The events of the novel and their coloring only peripherally involve the Civil War or any other familiar historical episode, yet the novel is historical in impact and intention. It is historical through Faulkner's careful construction of explicit parallels between his central figure, Joe Christmas, and the historical or mythic figure of Jesus Christ.

Christmas' historical character resides in his conscious choice to live his life as a black, to assume in contemptuous penance for original sin the full burden of blackness, despite the fact that his skin-color would allow him to pass as white. Whether Christmas is a mulatto in fact, genetically, is never unequivocally established; thus for him to choose blackness in Mississippi is a tragic choice, and a choice that lodges him firmly in history. Through Christmas, Faulkner establishes the historical isolation of the Negro from all phases of American life, not merely from southern village or city life. Christmas is one of the few characters in Faulkner's work to leave the South; he wanders north for a time, still cut off and still embittered, contemptuous, and triumphantly proud.

The narrative complexity of *Light in August* is rivaled only in *Absalom, Absalom!* (1936). It will suffice to note here the comparatively straightforward narrative of Christmas: his adoption from an orphanage and his harrowing upbringing by the Presbyterian McEacherns; his flight over a period of years; his arrival in Jefferson; the murder of Joanna Burden; the tracking down of Joe Christmas, his castration and death at the hands of the tin-horn hero, Percy Grimm. In parallel are the narratives of Lena Grove, pregnant and moving on foot through Alabama and Mississippi to find her scoundrel of a lover, Brown; Byron Bunch's Joseph-like love for Lena; and the looming, doomed, mad figure of Hightower, the voice of reason who identifies himself with his own grandfather in the Civil War.

The mythic pattern of the novel emerges from Faulkner's use of Biblical analogue, explicit or implicit. Although that pattern is necessarily conscious on Faulkner's part, it does not arouse our resistance, because it unfolds slowly, subtly, and seemingly naturally from the country speech and manner of Armstid and the itinerant furniture repairer who closes the novel, from the accumulation of detail, highly selected and absolutely right for the place and time. We learn of Joe Christmas' uncertain origins only in Chapter 6, one-fourth through the whole; Christmas is an orphan of uncertain parentage, appearing out of nowhere, like Moses, like the many heroes of myth. When McEachern takes the little boy, Joe Christmas, to his home, Mrs. McEachern washes his feet, an unmistakable allusion to John, 12:3, in which Mary, Lazarus' sister, washes Christ's feet. ("I done washed just yesterday," the little boy says.) [10] The adolescent Joe Christmas, born on Christmas day, learns in one of Faulkner's most powerful scenes, of sexuality, and of "woman filth": menstruation. The knowledge sends him, rifle on arm, to stalk and shoot a sheep, in the blood of which he bathes his hands (p. 174). The Christian symbolism of the blood of the sacrificial lamb at once anticipates Joe Christmas' fate and enforces Faulkner's historical intention. That symbolism is seemingly inverted through sacrilege, coming as it does after the group rape of a Negro girl in a barn; it is not inverted or sacrilegious, however, in that Joe refrains from his part in the group assault, his human and racial sensibilities in turmoil. The entire episode is astonishing. After his apparent murder of McEachern, Joe runs off for fifteen years, his years in the wilderness, years of anonymity; at age thirty-three, Christ's legendary age at His death, Joe Christmas endures his form of crucifixion. Brown, Lena Grove's seducer and Joe's accomplice in bootlegging, betrays Joe, Judas-like, in hopes of the $1,000 reward posted for the apprehension of Joanna Burden's murderer. The local mob, led by Percy Grimm, pursues Christmas, looking for "somebody to crucify"; they capture Christmas in Mottstown on a Friday.

Faulkner has been criticized for inconsistency in his use of Christian parallels. Lena Grove, Milly Hines (Joe's mother), and Mrs. McEachern can all be seen as the Virgin Mary, two too many. Mad old Hines, Joe's grandfather, becomes God the Father, an unsatisfactory identification at best; and Faulkner gives us too many Josephs: both McEachern and Byron Bunch, Lena's baby's surrogate father. Such objections are off the point if the novel is read with literary, rather than legal, intelligence. Faulkner's circular narration guides our perception; as the narrative folds back upon itself like a receding wave, the place of the past is insisted upon, and our minds are prepared seriously to accept Joe Christmas as a figural representation of Jesus Christ. Faulkner overcomes the banality of the identification by means of his narrative control; he produces the most harrowing novel, without exception, in modern fiction. He also gives us one further example of the urge on the part of the post-Romantic to leave the limitations of the immediately social for the freedom of myth. For Faulkner, however, the limitation of society is not really a limitation, but a source of strength. In *Light in August* he manages to give scope to his always powerful Christian imagination, but to keep matters in hand through his sharpness of perception, his extraordinary ability to bring country people to life on the page, and not least, through his knowledge of social life in its daily, tedious, manifestations.

In his best writing, Faulkner's strategy is to set up a disparity, comic or tragic, between the local, interior viewpoint upon a situation and the viewpoint of the figure who is strange to the local scene, or who, having left it to return, brings an exterior way of thought and vision to that scene. Two sets of values clash, and moral drama (to say nothing of operatic confrontation) results. What one might call the return-of-the-native device is common, even basic to the traditional novel, but particularly common to twentieth-century American novelists. Hemingway's fisherman in "Big, Two-Hearted River" is a returned native, as are Fitzgerald's Jay Gatsby and Dos Passos' World War I veterans in *USA;* Thomas Wolfe asserts of all his autobiographical central characters that they cannot go home again. The viewpoint of the returned native is particularly appropriate to the writer whose burden is historical, and in intent, tragic. It is the reverse of *Bildung*, the novel of ever-unfolding experience in which meaning derives from the process of education, a process that implies the likelihood of a better future, an optimistic idea of progress. In *The Sound and the Fury* it is Quentin Compson who leaves Jefferson to find a different perspective at Harvard. He returns to Mississippi not physically, but in his tortured mind, to become self-elected victim of his interior journey. Gavin Stevens, the Jefferson lawyer educated at Harvard and Heidelberg, returns literally, to comment, to listen, and as Faulkner's powers waned, to narrate. Structurally, the Snopes family, although utterly native, play a similar part: they and their principle of aggrandizement are foreign to what Faulkner sees as admirable in the South.

In *Light in August,* the returned native is of course Joe Christmas, but here his journey is almost as complex as Dante's in *The Divine Comedy.* Christmas makes a journey from whiteness to blackness, a racial journey in his conscious assumption of blackness. That journey can have no other destination than his lynching, for among the Negroes he is still "white folks," and his life among whites is summed up in his murder of Joanna Burden. He kills her for trying to force him into a middle-class black manner of life; she has tried, in short, to contain his outrage within a convention that he can see only as ludicrous. That journey is literal when Christmas runs the roads of the world out of Mississippi to the cities of the North, to New Mexico, then back, an outcast by choice, living as a day laborer or petty criminal. His journey is symbolic, as we have seen by the freight of religious meaning that Faulkner imposes through his Biblical emblems and analogues.

Above all, Joe Christmas' journey is historical. One must recall that after Christmas' capture by the mob at Mottstown, he is taken to Jefferson, where he escapes, seizes a pistol, and runs to the Reverend Gail Hightower's house. There Percy Grimm shoots and castrates Christmas. If any single chapter of the novel can be said to be the most important, it is the penultimate chapter (20) of *Light in August.* Following immediately upon Christmas' hideous death, we have the quiet narrative of Hightower's life, in the course of which Faulkner brings together all the historical and dramatic tangents of the complex work. An unfrocked clergyman, Hightower is obsessed by the Civil War, and with the death of his grandfather (also named Gail) in a futile cavalry raid on Jefferson, when late in the war it was a Yankee garrison town. The Reverend Hightower, an old man wounded by Christmas' pistol blow, reflects upon his family and his past, noting significantly that he has "skipped a generation" (p. 452). The grandfather was a whiskey-drinking, slave-owning bravo whose exploits, recounted by ex-slaves, delighted the little grandson. The Reverend Hightower's grandfather had been quite different from his flamboyant father; a clergyman, an antislavery man, he had served the Confederacy, a cause in which he did not believe, as a surgeon. To his son he was a wraith, a ghost, whose only effect was to direct the boy to the seminary.

Hightower's story, related so late in the novel, tends to usurp the story of Joe Christmas. It does not in fact do so, for it serves rather as a coda to the death of Christmas. Hightower is as symbolic as Christmas, but Faulkner's ability to lodge him firmly in society, to portray him in social and historical terms, permits and indeed directs the most critical reader to full belief. In his confusion and obsession, Hightower, dying, is the post-Civil War South. He honors his grandfather for a noble boy, crazed with hunger, carrying out the impossible cavalry raid with other boys in desperation and from boys' eagerness for a prank. At the same time, Hightower insists upon the point that his grandfather had no saber, was not an officer, as the old slave insisted, and that Gail Hightower was not killed in battle but was shot by a woman with a fowling piece as he raided a chicken coop. Nobility and indignity combine to historical truth. Still, as Hightower is dying, he again relives the cavalry raid:

It is as though they had merely waited until he could find something to pant with, to be reaffirmed in triumph and desire with, with this last left of honor and pride and life. He hears above his heart the thunder increase, myriad and drumming. Like a long sighing of wind in trees it begins, then they sweep into sight, borne now upon a cloud of phantom dust. They rush past, forwardleaning in the saddles, with brandished arms, beneath whipping ribbons from slanted and eager lances; with tumult and soundless yelling they sweep past like a tide whose crest is jagged with the wild heads of horses and the brandished arms of men like the crater of the world in explosion. They rush past, are gone; the dust swirls skyward sucking, fades away into the night which has fully come. Yet, leaning forward in the window, his bandaged head huge and without depth upon the twin blobs of his hands upon the ledge, it seems to him that he still hears them: the wild bugles and the clashing sabres and the dying thunder of hooves. [Pp. 466–467.]

Hightower is the South, divided in loyalty, rent by illusion at odds with reality, a walking, thinking, historical anomaly whose untidy death results from an almost accidental blow at the hand of a man self-loathing and self-proscribed.

Like Hermann Broch, Faulkner here is far distant from the mere use of history as a backdrop for staged effects. He portrays with imaginative sympathy the state of a society at a precisely defined point in human history. Again like Broch's in *Die Schlafwandler*, Faulkner's vision of history in *Light in August* is apocalyptic, but never, to use Novalis' word, only the work of a man turned "orator."

CHAPTER 5

The Anachronous Hero: Hemingway and Montherlant

Few of their readers would quarrel with the proposal that both Ernest Hemingway and Henry de Montherlant derive directly from historical Romanticism. Indeed, both writers serve for readers of Neoclassical turn of mind as horrid examples of what is wrong with Romanticism, whether historical or recent. Hemingway's and Montherlant's egotism and flamboyance offend; their obsession with war and violence tramples on whole areas of contemporary sensibility; their writing about the art of bullfighting is seen as the equivalent of hanging cats by their tails over a clothesline; their fondness for sport, together with their equivocal treatment of women, leads to charges of fascism, anti-intellectualism, and homosexuality. Each writer, having chosen suicide, is out of fashion in the years after his death, inhabiting a critical limbo, hastily glanced at when not simply disregarded. Each, however, is safe in his separate pantheon: Montherlant, an Academician toward the end, embalmed in the luxurious, india-paper volumes of the Pléiade; Hemingway with his Nobel Prize, his biographies official and unofficial, all equally subject to the legend of his glamor, his appetites, his illusions and delusions.

Literary journalists have often called Montherlant "the French Hemingway," to his intense dissatisfaction. He once made it clear to an interviewer (this writer) that he had never considered it necessary to read the American master, and that whereas he, Montherlant, had confronted living bulls in the plaza, Hemingway had merely written about the subject as a spectator. We have no evidence that Hemingway ever read Montherlant's work. The two never met. Despite Montherlant's disclaimer, the affinity between the two men (exact contemporaries) in attitude and sensibility is sufficiently profound to merit juxtaposition of them here.

Although Hemingway and Montherlant received in their lifetime a good deal of critical and uncritical discussion, neither has received the quality of attention that far inferior writers in both France and the United States customarily attract. Hemingway's official biographer, Carlos Baker, found it necessary to write a study entitled *Hemingway: The Writer as Artist,* thus reassuring all and sundry that Hemingway was indeed an artist rather than a torero or big-game hunter. The later official biography, ironically, is a blow-by-blow account of Hemingway's meals, drinks, loves and flirtations, in which Hemingway's place as a writer is barely alluded to, much less accounted for. As for Montherlant, more often than not, since World War II, remarks about his alleged pro-Nazism (mistaken remarks, in my view) have taken the place of genuine criticism of his imaginative work. Both writers have thus suffered from an excess of biographical interpretation, and each was guilty of encouraging the biographical excesses that have been committed upon him.

Let us disregard biography, insofar as possible, in the notion that speculation about Hemingway's alleged alcoholism or Montherlant's cornada in the lung of 1925 is less rewarding then a view of the two men in relation to their use, or misuse, of the historical theme. I begin with Hemingway, for although he appears simple and even simple-minded to skeptics, he is in truth more complex and difficult than is Montherlant, who is never accused of simple-mindedness. Because Hemingway's work was uneven in quality, it is first necessary to specify which Hemingway one has in mind. The Hemingway canon that I honor extends from *Three Stories and Ten Poems* (1923), *The Sun Also Rises* (1926), and *A Farewell to Arms* (1929), and through the collections of short stories of the twenties and thirties. It does not include *The Torrents of Spring* nor *Death in the Afternoon*, nor any novel after 1929, any of the World War II journalism, and certainly not *The Old Man and the Sea*. The posthumous publication of *A Moveable Feast* and of *Islands in the Stream* (1970) is a disservice if not dishonor to the memory of a fine writer.

Hemingway's best work, as indeed all his work, would seem, at first glance, to be as firmly lodged in history as William Faulkner's, or any other frankly "historical" writer in the Romantic or post-Romantic mode. Hemingway writes repeatedly of war and of warriors, and he frequently gives us the illusion that his warriors are living out their private histories in terms set for them by standard, public history. But is that really the case? Before one can consider the matter in greater detail, one must take up the matter of the famous Hemingway style, for within that style lies concealed the personal and public essence that made of Hemingway a writer in the first place.

On one side, we have Leon Edel's hostile remark that Hemingway is not first-rate because, along with Sinclair Lewis, he created only the illusion of a style rather than the reality. "A style involves substance as well as form . . . I would argue that Hemingway has not created a Style: he has rather created the artful illusion of a Style. . . . He has conjured up the effect of a Style by a process of evasion, very much as he sets up an aura of emotion—by walking directly away from emotions! . . . He has not written an 'adult' novel." [1]

For contrast, we have Hemingway's own generous account of his style in *Death in the Afternoon*. He compares a good style (his own) to an iceberg, seven-eighths under water, thus suggesting the writer's need to reach down, and through excision to discover the exactly right sequence of event, emotion, and word. The measure of truth in the description has been obscured for many readers by Hemingway's literary braggadocio here, by his implication that he was the only writer who taught himself style, the only writer who ever went hungry for his art. As for his event-emotion-word sequence, it is unduly behavioristic and oversimplified.

A more interesting, although oblique, analysis of style appears in the short story "Soldier's Home," one of Hemingway's best stories, and one which appeared in his first collection of stories, *In Our Time*. Young Krebs has returned from the war to his home town in Oklahoma only to find that no one wants to hear the dull truth about experience in combat. The townspeople have heard about so many atrocities that truth bores them. Like other returned soldiers, Krebs obliges with lies.

Krebs found that to be listened to at all he had to lie, and after he had done this twice, he, too, had a reaction against the war and against talking about it. A distaste for everything that had happened to him in the war set in because of the lies he had told. All of the times that had been able to make him feel cool and clear inside himself when he thought of them; the times so long back when he had done the one thing, the only thing for a man to do, easily and naturally, when he might have done something else, now lost their cool, valuable quality and then were lost themselves.

. . . .

Krebs acquired the nausea in regard to experience that is the result of untruth and exaggeration. . . .[2]

"Soldier's Home" ends with Krebs's mother indicating to him that his father thinks it time for his son to settle down and get a job. Krebs's blank reaction leads his mother to ask whether he loves her. He replies that he doesn't love anyone. She weeps, forces him to kneel with her, although he cannot pray. She pries from him the lie that he does love her. He feels sorry for her, "and she had made him lie." (p. 251). He will not work in his father's office, but will go to Kansas City for a job. In the meantime, he goes to the school grounds to watch his sister pitch indoor baseball, the small sister whom he indeed loves.

The conception not only of a literary style, but also of a way of life, far from a simple one, is assuredly here in the brief narrative. It is also present in more complex form in Hemingway's first two novels. In Krebs's thoughts, however, the enunciated conception is more simple than conveyed reality. Hemingway appears to confine Krebs, and himself, to "the times that had been able to make him feel cool and clear inside himself . . . the times so long back when he had done the one thing, the only thing for a man to do, easily and naturally, when he might have done something else. . . ." The impact of the story derives from the difference between Krebs's aspiration that his life run smoothly, with no more "consequences," and Hemingway's demonstration through inference that Krebs's life is and will continue to be steeped in complexity and necessary consequences. Hemingway's constant theme in his fiction, that the times are out of joint, is developed with finesse. After a hard war in the Marines, Krebs returns from the Rhineland in 1919, long after the local heroes, draftees all, have been celebrated. Krebs observes his parents and their conventional lives as though they were animals in a zoo; he has lost religious faith; he does not want to involve himself in the hypocritical ritual of courtship with the local girls. He opens up only to his tomboy sister, the pitcher: "How's the old wing?" (p. 248). The reality of the literary conception here is Proustian in its complexity, if we can admit a Proust whose first impulse is ethical rather than aesthetic.

The popular success of Hemingway's style, or styles, may be accounted for in his ability to project through style the illusion that complex matters of conscience and conduct can be reduced to elements, ordered, and so dominated. Hemingway gave that process an aura of perfection by polishing and rigorous control. In truth the style is limited and flawed, although the flaws are camouflaged and the limitations made to appear sources of strength. Unlike Faulkner's fiction, Hemingway's is outside, or beyond history. In his selection of character and incident, and in his prose style, the historical past cannot be evoked, not even through allusions to historical event. In place of history, Hemingway, like Proust, gives us memory, although Hemingway's use of memory is again camouflaged by the characters' strong emotion at discovering that the times are truly out of joint. Arcadia, the green and good place, is never far from the immediate fictional scene. Hemingway's style is contemporary without being local or provincial; this accounts for its freshness, and for its attraction for people who themselves lack a sense of history, or who do not want the writer to thicken his context by an appeal to the historical consciousness. By and large, Hemingway's world is the world of ever unfolding present, rather than past,

events, even though those events have occurred in narrative
time past. The following is from Chapter 10 of *The Sun Also
Rises:*

We all got in the car and it started up the white dusty road into Spain.
For a while the country was much as it had been; then, climbing all
the time, we crossed the top of a Col, the road winding back and
forth on itself, and then it was really Spain. There were long brown
mountains and a few pines and far-off forests of beech-trees on some
of the mountainsides. The road went along the summit of the Col
and then dropped down, and the driver had to honk, and slow up,
and turn out to avoid running into two donkeys that were sleeping
in the road. We came down out of the mountains and through an
oak forest, and there were white cattle grazing in the forest.[3]

The passage is characteristic of much that is memorable in
Hemingway's writing. It demonstrates his ability to infuse
vigor and emotion into passages which, in another writer,
might be only backdrop. We catch Jake Barnes's, the narrator's, passion for Spain, a passion which at the same time
underlines the flow of images in time present, despite the
narrator's use of narrative time past. Emotion and event in
time present are by nature antihistorical.

A related antihistorical device is the use of the first-per-
son narrator. Although that device imparts vividness and
ensures the reader's involvement, the narrator keeps us in the
flow of the present, rigidly within the dramatic unfolding of
the narrative; we are not allowed to range into the historical
past. (Fifty years after *The Sun Also Rises,* our antihistorical
bias is proved by the widespread elimination from fiction of
the narrator, with his illusion of time past, in favor of narrative time present.) Hemingway used the techniques of the
short story upon the novel, a form traditionally within and in
an essential way about history. He occasionally alludes to
actual, historical people and events, as in *The Sun Also Rises*

when he introduces the toreros, Juan Belmonte and Marcial Lalanda. Their historicity, however, violates the careful illusion of reality, and the reader is conscious of the bump of the violation. Hemingway's narrators, particularly Frederick Henry of *A Farewell to Arms*, are placed in the impossible position of having to narrate their own heroism. Their position is impossible, for both Henry and Jake Barnes are decent, reticent men rather than blowhards. Aware of the difficulty, Hemingway tempers his frankly heroic characters' accounts with humor and understatement. Still one may be put off by their knowingness, their oppressive expertise. Frederick Henry knows weapons, wines, food, cities, architecture, painting, languages, surgery, tactics and strategy, bartenders, the Italian aristocracy, horses, and details of the coastline of Lago Maggiore in the dark. As a result he ought to be insufferable; it is a tribute to Hemingway that for many readers, Henry remains sympathetic to the end.

If style works against one's disposition to read either *The Sun Also Rises* or *A Farewell to Arms* in terms of the history of the event central to both novels, World War I, then by the time of *For Whom the Bell Tolls* (1940), Hemingway would seem to have recognized the difficulty. That novel is narrated by the omniscient writer rather than in the first person, and it appears to address history directly, to be a discourse on one of the central events of the century, the Spanish Civil War. In reality, however, *For Whom the Bell Tolls* is as a-historical as any other novel of Hemingway's; what we find is not a consciousness rooted in history in the person of Robert Jordan, but a series of existential moments, often skillfully evoked, sometimes not, but never historical. The sense of issues, of ideology, which after all dominated the Spanish struggle, is missing, and Hemingway's characters have reality only in personal, not in public terms. A Spanish reviewer wrote of Hemingway with wit, accuracy, and cruelty, "Oyó campanas sin saber exactamente donde" (literally, "He heard bells without knowing exactly where from").[4] The novel takes place in a heroic never-never land of pine forests, compliant girls in sleeping bags, and bridges there for the blowing.

What, then, of Montherlant? Hemingway and Montherlant not only write of the same subject matter—the transition from youth to manhood, war, bullfighting, sport, and sex—they also share the conviction that the times are out of joint, and that heroes, however anachronous, exist. Above all, they share a common attitude toward experience, one that Montherlant evokes in the mind of his hero, Alban de Bricoule of *Le Songe* and other novels: "O monde, je veux ce que tu veux. Tout ce qui arrive arrive justement."[5] ("Oh world, I want what you want. Whatever happens, happens appropriately.") That attitude is also expressed repeatedly in Montherlant's fiction and journals by his determination "être dans le vrai," or "être dans le réel" ("to exist only in reality, in the area of truth"). Such an attitude would seem to contradict the notion that the times are out of joint; it rather complements it. Recognition of fact belongs to "être dans le vrai"; it also reflects an attitude toward nature. The characteristic hero of both writers, Alban de Bricoule, Pierre Costals, Auligny, Robert Jordan, Frederick Henry, or Jake Barnes, displays an effort to live in nature, to accept nature, and a parallel effort to oppose nature and to impose an unnatural order upon nature. In the process, Hemingway is a-historical; Montherlant is historical.[6]

Although they are seven years apart in time, Montherlant's *Le Songe* (1922) and Hemingway's *A Farewell to Arms* (1929) cry out for comparison. Both novels are about the war, but neither is a "war novel" as that uncritical phrase is usually understood. Both writers' subject is the residue of experience in war rather than the immediate trauma of war;

how subsequent experience cannot be conceived of as experience until it is extreme. In both *Le Songe* and *A Farewell
to Arms* we find an interesting insistence upon the extremity
of experience in time of war, an anachronistic conception of
the heroic, and careful attention to the context of the specific
experience in order to create sympathy for characters who,
without such attention, might appear ludicrous. Neither novel
has a plot.

Hemingway begins *in medias res* with Frederick Henry
in the ambulance service, attached to the Italian army on the
Austrian front. He is wounded during an attack, sent to Milan
to recover, where he has a passionate affair with the Scottish
nurse, Catherine Barkley, and upon his recovery is ordered to
the front again. In the retreat from Caporetto, Henry deserts,
joins the now pregnant Catherine, and makes his way with
her to Switzerland, where she dies in childbirth.

Montherlant first presents Alban de Bricoule in Paris in
the middle of the war. Because of recent unsuccessful minor
surgery, he has been assigned to noncombatant duty in Paris,
but he "envies" his Lycée classmates their deaths and determines to volunteer for duty in a regiment at the front. We also
meet Dominique Soubrier, a young athlete in whom Alban is
interested. She returns his interest warmly and comes to fall
in love with him after he has gone to the front as an infantry-
man, and she to duty as a nurse in a hospital not far behind
the lines. The bulk of the narrative has to do with Alban's
reaction to combat, to his comrades, and to himself, whom he
observes with chilling objectivity. He humiliates Dominique
in the course of a cruelly comic assignation, and he returns to
his unit at the front.

Banal in outline, neither novel is so. Hemingway's distinction, and his limitation, is that he sacrifices so much to
the creation of drama. Character for Hemingway is a product

of drama and is revealed through action. The significant exception, however, occurs in the scenes between Henry and the priest, scenes in which Hemingway develops the religious theme beyond the limits of mere drama. One could indeed assert that Hemingway's imagination is always religious rather than historical. Within Hemingway's own conventions, Frederick Henry is a fully developed character, but it comes as a surprise to learn, some three-quarters of the way through, that he had studied architecture in Rome. At that, Hemingway tells us that fact only because of the demands of the narrative. Hemingway's technique makes inordinate demands upon dialogue and description, since he forbids himself any manner of psychological analysis. The pressure of those demands accounts for his notorious mannerisms and invites the accusation of simple-mindedness. Beneath it all, his attitude to war is one of fascinated horror. He appears to say that desertion is proper because war is indeed hell; a statement that implies an ethical judgment if not moral revulsion at the prospect of involvement in war. Such revulsion, however, is contradicted when Hemingway's descriptions of military action are so perfect, so clearly the product of his perception of the processes of war, indeed of his loving fascination with them, that process as such encroaches enormously upon psychological meaning or moral implication: the novel finally seems, paradoxically, a novelette. This is to say that Hemingway's conception of drama is insufficient to sustain the intellectual burden that the subject and the writer's irony encourage us to perceive.

Montherlant, on the other hand, stands firmly within the great French tradition of psychological analysis. Montherlant's originality lies in his thought, his loathing for received opinion, and in his disdain for fashion, but not in departure from long-honored literary tradition. His formal conception is

closer to the eighteenth century of Choderlos de Laclos than
to the twentieth century of Gide, Camus, or Sarraute. As in all
his fiction, in *Le Songe* attitudes toward experience are crystal
clear, intellectually enunciated; and drama, the stuff of the
novel, is invented only to support an enunciated position. A
few pages into *Le Songe*, accordingly, we know exactly where
we are: Alban not only "envies" his friends their deaths, he
finds extraordinary virtues in war itself (Hemingway does
too, although before the frightful Colonel Cantwell of *Across
the River and into the Trees* he does not fully admit it).
Early in the novel before Alban has been in combat, he muses
about what life at the front must be:

> "A dugout, a place of misery, of death— But all purified, simpli-
> fied! The simplicity of action, above all the action of war! If I were
> to establish any degree of intellectual or social influence, what pa-
> tience, labor, how many stumbling-blocks in my way, what clever-
> ness—and I would be criticized, not supported, by those whom I
> love; my best friends might become my adversaries; and who could
> reassure me that I would be living an authentic existence [dans le
> vrai], deliver me from doubt? But here! To stand at the parapet, to
> go have a look and come back, to pull a trigger, that is something
> clear, direct, that upon the moment may confer a splendid glory.
> Here values are rated, classified; everyone knows what they are.
> What superiority! What peace!" [Pp. 9–10.]

Like many of Montherlant's characters, Alban displays here
the intellectual's lust for the unequivocal, for a certainty that
such persons can find only in situations of extremity, whether
war, sport, or bullfighting. It is Montherlant's form of irony
that Alban's precious musings, based on intuition rather than
knowledge, are not punctured by experience at the front. They
are rather sustained, and we begin to see that Montherlant
is constructing a "superior" man derived by way of Barrès
from Nietzsche.[7]

In his admiration for Dominique as athlete, Alban discovers "the irreconcilable opposition between the order of sport and the order of the heart" (p. 21), an opposition that most, if not all Hemingway's central figures also experience. Alban leaves for the front with a sense of relief, glad to leave Dominique, seeing the life of action as "awash in the elemental, the annihilation of mind and heart" (p. 21), a phrase that sounds like an echo of the Spanish Foreign Legion's grotesque "Abajo la inteligencia. Arriba la muerte." ("Down with intelligence. Long live death.") On his way to the front, Alban remembers walking along the tramway to the football field, drops of water falling upon him from the trees, mud underfoot, and above all, the anticipation of not having to think, "ne pas penser!" once the game began.

Not to have to cover up the gaps in his education and the weakness of his mind, not to have to give reasons for his judgments, not to have to be critical; to contradict oneself, to be incoherent! the thousands of questions on which one had no opinion! [P. 30.]

Sport is the reverse of all that, and so is warfare, in which "Knowledge and intelligence and genius burn in a splendid auto da fé!" (p. 30). Once at the front, Alban joins his friend Prinet. Prinet says, "It is bad, here." Alban answers "avec hauteur, "Would you have me submit myself to mediocre tests?" (p. 31).

After he has been under fire for the first time, Alban reflects that

"When the whistling of the artillery barrage came down on me, and when at any moment I might be blasted into eternity, I had not a single religious thought, nor did I repent a single action, nor had I any impulse toward those whom I love." Since the day he had decided to go to the front, he had not once been taken by the idea of death; he had written to no one, nor had he made his will. [P. 76.]

The theme of pride in self-determination is expanded in a scene between Alban and Dominique, who has sought him out just behind the lines. She asks when he will return from the front lines, and he answers: in two days. Dominique responds,

"May fate [fatalité] bring it about."
"What!" he said, bristling because he had caught her out in the crime of failing to be intelligent, "I am here at my own request, by my own decision and obstinacy, and you call that fate! It is my will that constitutes fate . . . anyway, I am not going to die; my passions will keep me firmly on this earth. But after all, what a lot of tales about death! Why mourn because you are going to meet Plato and Marcus Aurelius again! I have admired all that is noble; there is no pleasure that I have not known; I have known happiness, too, genuine happiness— After that, I shall not be shocked if I am obliged to give up the game. I have gorged my hunger." [P. 89.]

The central statement of Montherlant's neo-stoicism occurs in a conversation between Alban and Prinet, in a trench. Prinet asks if Alban would really give up his life if it were demanded of him:

"I would do it, if I had to—by the sacraments that I received yesterday morning! I would not know the point of my sacrifice, but on the whole I think that I would be sacrificing myself to something that is nothing, that is only one of the illusions that I hate. Believing my sacrifice useless, and perhaps insane, without a witness, without desire, renouncing life and the sweet odor of humanity, I would throw myself into the indifference of the future only out of pride at having been so free. In the *Iliad*, Diomedes hurls himself upon Aeneas, although he knows that Apollo has rendered Aeneas invulnerable. Hector predicts the ruin of his city, his wife's imprisonment, before returning to fight as though he believed in victory. When the horse with the gift of prophecy announces to Achilles his approaching death, 'I am fully aware of it,' the hero answers. But instead of crossing his arms and awaiting death, he flings himself back and kills still more men in battle. That is how I have lived, knowing the vanity of things, but acting as though I were their dupe, and playing at being a man in order not to be rejected as a god. Yes, let us lose one in the other — my indifference and that of the future! After having pretended to be ambitious when I was not, to fear death when I did not fear it, having pretended to wait when I waited for nothing, I shall die in pretending to believe that my death has a purpose, but persuaded that it serves nothing and proclaiming that all is just." [Pp. 110–111.]

This recalls Hemingway's similar kind of rhetoric, his pastiche of a set of rules for medieval knightly combat which is his epigraph for the collection of short stories, *Winner Take Nothing* (1933): "the winner shall take nothing; neither his ease, nor his pleasure, nor any notions of glory; nor if he win far enough, shall there be any reward within himself." Hemingway thus defines the ideal of life that Montherlant called "service inutile," service without point in the absence of any manner of belief.[8]

Montherlant apparently sets himself the task of urging his reader to accept as heroic young Alban de Bricoule, a monster of egotism and absurdity, posing in the guise of Homeric hero, inhumanly conscious and approving of his own every thought and breath. Unlike Hemingway, Montherlant is not interested in making his characters charming; he prefers to outrage us. He portrays as admirable those impulses that our civilization says are evil: approval of warfare, of egotism, of the most antisocial attitudes. Montherlant does not pause there, however. He also describes a range of human reactions within Bricoule that come as welcome surprise. Alban's fine, human pity at the death of a German prisoner of war denies Alban's egotism and his philosophical preening. When his comrade Prinet is missing in action, Alban's vow "not to use his intelligence for three years" becomes an

amusing combination of the human and the inhuman. That
vow is at odds, however, with the basic philosophical position that Alban tries to maintain throughout; it is best summarized when Alban learns that Prinet has indeed been killed.
He momentarily resents the fact that he, Alban, suffers at the
knowledge of his friend's death, while external nature is
indifferent. Then he accuses himself of sentimentality:
"Foolish pronouncements about *the indifference of nature!*
What do we expect? That the trees shall drop their leaves
every time a human being dies?" (p. 165). Thus Alban lulls
his grief, finally telling himself, "O monde, je veux ce que tu
veux. Tout ce qui arrive arrive justement" (p. 166). In this
manner, Alban maintains his earlier position, the very Mon-
therlantian position of willing the inevitable. From the outset, Alban has asserted the primacy of his will: to Dominique
about volunteering for the front lines; to Prinet on the same
subject; and to himself throughout. Alban wills himself into
the war rather as Frederick Henry wills himself out of it.

In the final episodes of the novel, however, we discover
a complete reversal of field in Alban's responses, what Montherlant called "alternance" to identify his personal philosophy; it is at once identifiable as that highly Romantic
philosophy of polarities, deriving directly from Swedenborg
by way of Ralph Waldo Emerson.[9] Immediately after Alban's
lyrical acceptance of events ("Tout ce qui arrive arrive
justement"), German bombers arrive to work over the French
positions, and Alban is horrified to find himself in a state of
terror, craven with cowardice. He violates all his proud
virtues. He prays, he makes extravagant vows, he promises
God that he will endow entire communities if only he is
spared. He imagines himself dead, a corpse like Prinet. Then
comes the ultimate self-betrayal: he will do anything to be
evacuated from the line. He will lie, cheat, murder if need

be, anything to save his skin. The bombers break off the attack, and in the morning, as Alban's comrades take tally of the wounded and killed among them, he turns himself in to the field hospital with a superficial wound that he had received days earlier, and has no difficulty in being evacuated. The novel ends where it began, with the ambiguous affair between Alban and Dominique. Alban finally rejects her, seeing her as an Iphigenia, a sacrifice to save a soldier's life as he returns to the front. Thus the contrast to the conclusion to A *Farewell to Arms*, to the excessively neat death of both Catherine Barkley and her infant.

Le Songe, a very young man's novel, is much flawed; brief quotation and translation from it are unkind to Montherlant. It may not therefore be sufficiently clear that both he and Hemingway arrive at similar positions through different, but parallel, avenues. Each has an apocalyptic vision of the modern world that he creates and relives through the experience of warfare. Hemingway's prose style, with its vividness and its visual character, is superior, however, to Montherlant's lyricism, his highly charged *beau style* at odds with his matter. Partly because of the deceptive simplicity of his style, partly because of his apocalyptic vision, and partly because of idiosyncrasy, Hemingway has been widely accused of being anti-intellectual. And so he is, although his anti-intellectualism is based upon a highly intellectual apprehension of experience. In the case of Montherlant, his use of classical allusion, his extensive psychological analysis, his choice of an intellectual for hero, all would seem to deny the charge of anti-intellectualism. He remains, however, at least as anti-intellectual as Hemingway. His anti-intellectualism is of that pure Romantic variety that substitutes instinct for rationality and places blind faith in the superiority of art to any other pursuit.

The two writers agree about the place of nature in relation to human affairs, although they appear to disagree on the evidence of *Le Songe* and *A Farewell to Arms*. Where young Bricoule reminds himself that the leaves will not fall from the trees for any man's death, Frederick Henry sees a conspiracy on the part of the universe to kill off the good. Both in *A Farewell to Arms* and in the rest of his fiction, however, Hemingway allies the best of times, the best of people, and nature. Lyricism and happiness attach to nature and to activities pursued in nature: hunting, fishing, lovemaking — rather than in society. On the evidence of *Les Bestiaires* (1929) and *La Rose de sable* (written in the early thirties but withheld from full publication until 1967–1968),[10] Montherlant agreed with that juxtaposition, although he disguised his Romanticism with intellection and irony. Both writers pose the question of action versus contemplation, and both choose action as superior to contemplation, which of course is the Romantic choice. Both devise heroes who seek out extremes of experience, who live most fully when their lives are mortally threatened. For both writers, next to death itself, love in the virtually pathological form of eroticism is fundamental to their conception of relations between men and women. For both writers, their ultimate Romanticism lies in the frequent conjunction in their work of eroticism and death. That conjunction is less Wagnerian than it is proto-Existentialist, for it is a concentration upon experience for its own sake, as against social experience, or experience having results beyond the superior individual's own consciousness. For the eroticist, love becomes aggrandizement of self and assertion of the individual will, as opposed to a merging of wills in which the individual will is gratefully abandoned. Both Hemingway and Montherlant, therefore, may be described as Byronic-Nietzschean in their Romanticism, never Wordsworthian.

Although Hemingway and Montherlant share a post-Romantic apprehension of individuality, of the superiority of men who subject themselves to ultimate tests, and a conviction of apocalypse, they differ vividly in their relationship to history. Alban de Bricoule as hero is close to a Hemingway anachronous hero, but *Le Songe*, in its totality as novel reflecting a sense of history, differs significantly from any of Hemingway's novels.[11] As idiosyncratic as Alban de Bricoule is, one still knows that he has a past, that he has grown up in a specific society at a specific time, and that his denunciation of society is still a product of his having been subjected to manners and mores. Montherlant not only forcefully implies the existence of society, he convincingly suggests the historical fact of that society in crisis. He does so symbolically, early in the novel when Alban, thinking of the war, hears the growling of the panthers in the zoo, nearby his house (p. 10). Montherlant conveys the sense of an entire society responding to war through Dominique, through facts and suggestions about her life that combine to give historical depth. Frederick Henry, by contrast, seems to come out of nowhere and to be returning to nowhere. Society is neither presented nor implied; in its place are moving evocations of landscape and of individual responses to event. Hemingway's heroes, to repeat, move in an eternal present of vivid action; they have religious but not historical motivation.

Montherlant, as opposed to Hemingway, further achieves historical resonance through his constant use of classical allusion. His classical allusions are not the echoes, tags, and pastiche of Neo-Classicism. They are rather allusions chosen to support historically Romantic attitudes, as in the allusion to *The Iliad* quoted above. Alban not only finds a parallel to his own stoicism in recounting the responses of Diomedes in impossible positions; Alban also conveys by his responses the notion of human, therefore historical continuity. The times that are out of joint for Hemingway's characters are their own times only. The times that are out of joint for Montherlant date from the high tide of the Roman Empire.

History nevertheless is merely adumbrated in *Le Songe*. In *La Rose de sable*, which Montherlant called his first "objective" novel,[12] history is fully and inescapably present. Montherlant as historian and as prophetic artist combined to arrive at the theme of French colonialism in North Africa. His treatment of this theme caused Montherlant to withhold his work from full publication for thirty-five years; first because in 1932 the Italians threatened Tunis, and second because of the Algerian War following World War II. Montherlant wrote that, having taken the part of the indigenous peoples against the French, he did not want to embarrass his country at times of crisis.[13] Episodic and apparently formless, the novel really possesses a tight thematic form that may be summed up as the relationship between two kinds of power: armed military force and the force of eroticism. Montherlant portrays two apparently opposing principles of life in his two main characters: Lieutenant Auligny, a bourgeois in the professional army who goes out to Morocco in the hope of advancing his career, an *honnête homme* who awakens to the power of sex through his prolonged affair with Ram, a young Bedouin girl, and to the life of politics through his awareness of the injustices perpetrated upon the natives by the French. Guiscart, the opposing central figure, is an artist, a scoffing superior man, an aristocrat, and altogether a nasty piece of work. He is the judge of events, a man who harbors no doubts, in contrast to Auligny, and finally in ultimate crisis a craven savior of his own skin. Montherlant moves by description of specific scenes, people, and things, in episodes that are without logical connection, although progressively their interior logic becomes apparent. He walks around his subject, giving us a variety of points of view through epigram, satire, and psychological analysis. Montherlant is thus like Musil in technique; apparent formlessness disguises a remarkable intellectual control of the material.

The historical as opposed to the merely political theme is proposed in Montherlant's epigraph from Lyautey, an analytical and prophetic statement to the effect that France is in moral crisis, "surtout en Indochine," by its willingness to consider non-Europeans as inferior; that condescension gives birth to hatred and to the revolutions of the future. The historical theme is expanded in Montherlant's "objective" footnotes, as when he quotes a contemporary Deputy on French intervention in Algeria: "We rob the Dey. He protests. Then we shoot him" (p. 19). In its brevity and point, this might be Montherlant's own definition of colonialism. Montherlant's historical vision is given authenticity, however, by his awareness of the ambiguities involved in the French occupation of Morocco, by his knowledge that gray rather than black and white is the prevailing moral color.

Auligny, for example, committed to the Moroccans to the point of treason, notices a French sergeant leaning over an Arab, twisting the Arab's fingers in what seems a form of torture. Upon investigating, Auligny finds that the sergeant is helping the Arab to remove a ring that is too small. Auligny suggests soap; the ring is removed. The Arab then puts back the ring on the same finger, smiling (pp. 458–459). Auligny's vacillation, his increasing awareness of complexity, present and historical, make him increasingly a convincing, if not entirely sympathetic character. It is its aura of intellectual and psychological complexity, wedded to the historical theme, that gives the novel its stature. That mixture of the personal and the public is characteristically expressed as Auligny

learns of a proposed operation by the French against the
Bedouin, and is moved to protest illness in order not to take
part. To leave would resolve his doubts about Ram, his
exasperating, apathetic mistress; his colonel gives permission
for Auligny to telephone to Tamghist, the staging area, for his
replacement. Montherlant intervenes:

If an intelligent man cannot entirely believe in a situation because
he always sees contradictory reasons, reasons which always exist
and are always compelling, an unintelligent man who believes, he
too has his times of doubt. It is probable that even a saint is now
sustained and now humbled by doubts of his own charity. But that
man who has believed and who doubts, the mass of what he has
believed behind him and pushing him on, that man must advance
blindly, renouncing more and more the use of his wits, applying
fixative to a fugitive moment of continual mobility. Thus the way of
the world, and as a result, thus the average mind, lacking honesty
or courage, who wants what the world wants. And the man of duplicity succeeds the man of faith; one might even say that duplicity
emerges from faith, is a natural product of it. Matters stood differently
for Auligny. He had believed. Then he doubted. Ah, well, the thought
exalted him that his sacrifice was completely useless, even with
respect to Ram, who did not understand it, useless with respect to
the natives, among whom he was a stranger. He perceived the absurd
and took it for the good: one had been brought up to the morality
of honor and to Christian morality. When he had reached an altitude
where his act seemed infinitely pure and wasted, all the more pure
in proportion to its futility, his elevation induced in him a kind of
vertigo, and it was in that state of transport that he lifted the telephone receiver and called Tamghist. [Pp. 461–462.]

This scene gains perspective from our knowledge that Montherlant has reversed by 180 degrees his heroic pronounce-
ment of *Le Songe,* "O monde, Je veux ce que tu veux. . . ."

Auligny's vacillation is resolved for him by orders to
Fez. There he is betrayed to a rioting mob by one of the Arabs
whom he has tried to protect; abandoned by Guiscart, who

sets out to save his own skin; and slain. In the process of showing us Auligny as weak, idealistic, self-seeking, and unheroic, Montherlant makes his character both appealing and historical, for he establishes the vacillations of history itself, the difficulty of ascertaining truth in events and of assigning ultimate responsibility for decisions.

Hemingway's characters, so vivid and positive, cannot convey the sense of mess and indecision that pervades *La Rose de sable;* hence they lack historical possibility, as that term appears in Emil Staiger's "Der Zeitgeist und die Geschichte": "True historical thought with respect both to the past and to the future is undogmatic, unfettered, drunk with possibility." [14] Hemingway resists abstraction, and because of that resistance, he defies history, which in part is a process of abstracting and generalizing from particulars. Hemingway's series of personal moments are not historical, as Montherlant's are and Proust's are, because the drunkenness with possibility is not present. That is not to say that Hemingway is therefore aesthetically inferior to Montherlant; he is not. It is to say that the two writers differ significantly in ways that may not be obvious, for all their resemblances. [15]

CHAPTER 6

André Malraux

In the novels of André Malraux as in the person of that perplexing writer, many, if not all, the themes of the preceding chapters of this volume are clearly apparent. As with Hemingway and Montherlant, it is hardly necessary to argue the case for Malraux's position as a post-Romantic writer. Malraux's prophetic instinct for the typological violence of the twentieth century led him to Indochina a generation before the United States' involvement; he observed and wrote about the origins of the Chinese Revolution years before Mao had been heard of in the West; Malraux was in Madrid in July, 1936, when the Spanish Civil War broke out, and his activity on behalf of the Loyalists was as valuable as that of a trained brigade; his awareness of Nazism was vivid, as we know from *Les Temps du mépris* (1935), at a time when a heavy majority both in Europe and the United States was still hoping that, like a bad dream, the Nazis would simply go away. Malraux's activity first as a private in the Tank Corps, then as a colonel in the Resistance produced, before Hiroshima, *Les Noyers de l'Altenburg* (1943), in which the scene of the Germans experimenting with mustard gas on the Russians prophesies the atomic horror to follow.

Like Montherlant, Malraux does not conform, and has

never conformed, to fixed, logical political roles. He worked
for the Communist party from about 1926 to the Russo-German
pact in 1939, but all the while he was under attack as a dilet-
tante, as an individualist, too subject, in Trotsky's words, to
aesthetic caprice.[1] Malraux never in fact joined the Communist party. After the war, Malraux's association with De Gaulle
brought him attack from all quarters. He was seen as a conser-
vative reactionary, the classical radical in youth who turns
reactionary in his middle age; as a fascist, thirsty for power,
unprincipled, willing to wade wherever the stream of power
might wander. These facts are well known, but it is useful to
review them because as for Hemingway in his lifetime, so
for Malraux, his fame, the public role he flaunts, forces us to
consider nonliterary, indeed antiliterary aspects of his career,
even though we might wish to make an exclusively literary
judgment. Unlike Hemingway, Malraux has kept his private
life to himself, not even in his *Antimémoires* (1967) letting
slip pulp for the gossip mills.

Novelists of Malraux's acknowledged power and originality always run the risk of being misunderstood by readers
and critics alike. That Malraux has indeed been misread
seems clear. Whoever reads Malraux in English reads through
a cloud of mistranslation and omission of substantive matter.
Another large group of readers has been put off Malraux by
his reputation as a political partisan. So fine a novel as *L'Espoir*
(1937), therefore, is less well known than the fictional froth
of Colette, or the lesser novels of Sinclair Lewis. *Les Noyers
de l'Altenburg*, incomplete and fragmentary as it is, has been
virtually ignored, even though it is a fragment of unusual
intellectual acuity and emotional force. More than the fiction
of any other modern writer, more than Faulkner's, or Broch's
or Thomas Mann's, Malraux's fiction constitutes an *œuvre*, a
unified work, even though each novel is complete unto it-

self. Each work contains the next; each later work comments upon the former. The trilogy *La Lutte avec l'ange*, of which *Les Noyers de l'Altenburg* is the first part, has never, alas, been published. In every portion of Malraux's *œuvre*, in every novel and virtually in every scene of every novel, the conception at work has immediate and primary meaning in history; it derives from history and it comments upon history.

I would insist on Malraux's historical vision at the outset of this discussion, because French criticism deriving from phenomenology has induced miscomprehension of Malraux that far exceeds the linguistic or the political.[2] Such criticism was long fashionable in France and abroad; it remains powerful despite its inaccuracies long after its vogue has passed. Jeanne Delhomme, for example, in *Temps et destin: Essai sur André Malraux* (1955) gave her book a long epigraph that begins with a quotation from *Les Noyers de l'Altenburg*, the famous exchange between Möllberg and Vincent Berger:

> "We may imagine man's permanence, but it would be permanence in nothingness." [Möllberg.]
> "Or in the fundamental?" [Berger.]

> Andre Malraux's thought is situated between that affirmation and that question; in answers to traditional metaphysics which is no more than a positivistic view of existence, to the summary ontology which is no more than a positivism of the absolute, Malraux extracts the question of the *fundamental*, beyond the generality of particular beings, of the world and of existence, but from which particular beings neither the world nor being can be separated.[3]

Mlle Delhomme's entire book is written in the tortured and opaque rhetoric of her epigraph. Her prose is such, one suspects, because of the effort required to pry from their contexts key phrases and concepts, as when Mlle Delhomme denies the idea of historical time in the Möllberg-Berger exchange in favor of a mythic "eternal return." [4] She is correct in placing that exchange at the center of Malraux's work, however. The discussion between the two men, Berger a humanist, Möllberg a vaguely Spenglerian type, relates to the question of whether man has a basic human essence, or whether modern civilizations existing in history and in time, deprived of the illusion of eternal life, produce man dominated by fatality, by *le néant*, nullity.

It is true that Malraux's diction invites the Existentialist interpretation, but as Joseph Frank has pointed out, it is an error to fail to perceive that Malraux anticipates rather than echoes the Existentialist phrase, and that only peripherally, not centrally.[5] In his earliest novel, *Les Conquérants* (1928), as well as in all the later fiction, ultimate situations, deliberations on the nature of human freedom, on the role of the will (Nietzschean, not Existentialist),[6] on the phenomenon of human isolation in love and death, are prominent. Such recurrent themes and motifs are so prominent that the postwar joy of the Existentialist critics in their new recruit, Malraux, is comprehensible. Their reading was faulty, however, not only because it was antihistorical, but also because it omitted an essential step in our logical comprehension of Malraux: it omits the Romantic step, and such an omission is like knowing that there was one more, or one less, step at the bottom of the stairway than one's ganglia were prepared for.

The notion of Malraux as a post-Romantic takes us back to my earlier discussion concerning the self in relation to society. When discussing Hermann Broch, I noted that in an ordered society, one of accepted hierarchies, the individual is assigned his role; that individual accepts, or rejects, his identity in terms of that role, and though he may not be happy in his role, he knows who he is and where he is. When the social structure falls apart, the conception of role falls apart too. Identity in the old sense, automatic identity, ceases to exist, and we have the process, rich for literature, in which the individual must strip the self bare in order to reinvent the self. Pure identity comes into being as the rock bottom, the basis of survival. I further suggested that that is the post-Romantic guise, that is the point at which we see Broch's central characters, Pasenow and Esch in particular; and to a degree it may well be at the center of Musil's quest through the character of Ulrich, and ironically through Moosbrugger.

In his attempt at orientation, the Romantic individual has for raw materials himself and nature, and nature, as in the case of Wordsworth, contains both "disturbance and equilibrium," both "disorientation and orientation." The Romantic artist may find in nature, particularly if he is a transcendentalist, a source of redemption, and if he is a Christian, he will insist upon a principle of redemption in some region beyond society itself. If he is not a Christian, if he is an atheist, like Proust and Musil and Malraux, he will attach even greater value to the self; he will be enormously conscious of the self in relation to history and to phenomena. He may be suspended in that state of "negative Romanticism" as identified by Morse Peckham.[7]

The question that Möllberg and Vincent Berger debate, the question of the "fundamental" nature of human beings, is none other than the great Romantic question that has been debated for the past two hundred years. Early German Romantics abandoned the question, or like Friedrich Schlegel, they answered it by becoming converted to Roman Catholicism. Others discovered the "fundamental" in art, indeed, in a later generation, in the belief in *l'art pour l'art;* still others, like Faulkner, in history, or in history conceived as myth; others, in awareness—full, exquisite, horrible, of the possibilities

and probabilities of the self in all manner of situation, historical or unhistorical. In this latter area we may locate both
Hemingway and Malraux: the one, Hemingway, dubious of
history, even afraid of it, constructing his work out of his
unacknowledged but very real fear. The other, Malraux,
wonderfully and prophetically aware of history, equally dubious, perhaps, but capable of locating the human self, without the help of God or of the gods, in history.

Peckham writes of the Romantic sense of history, that
from the "percept of the self as the source of order flows
Romanticism's essentially antimetaphysical character. With
and without the aid of Kant, an orientation is now seen not as
a discovery but as a projection. Thus a metaphysical theory
is thought of as an instrument, not as a reality, not as something in Nature, but as something imposed upon it. On the
one hand it is conceived as an instrument for symbolizing th
self or value; on the other it is thought of as an epistemologic
instrument. Further consequences flow from this. If an orientation is only instrumentally, not constitutively, valid, it is
useful only temporarily. But then value, identity, and order
can be experienced only temporarily, in moments of illumination, spots of time. Further, the Romantic knows from history,
his own and man's, that the great human temptation is to regard an orientation as final and that succumbing leads to
disaster, for Christianity and Enlightenment had ultimately
collapsed. Consequently his moral task is to break down an
orientation once it has been fully realized. His only means
is self-disorientation. Hence the judgment often made that the
Romantic values emotional disturbance for its own sake. Not
at all; he values it as a means to break down an orientation,
which, as a human being, he is tempted to preserve but as a
Romantic human being, he knows by definition is inadequate.
As Browning implied, the only failure is success. Hence

throughout the nineteenth century the use of drugs, alcohol, sex, and Asiatic theologies as means of deliberately dislocating the senses so that new worlds may emerge. Only with the breakthrough into modern art did the Romantic artist and thinker learn how to break down an orientation without partially disintegrating his personality." [8]

The central point, here, that "the Romantic knows from history, his own and man's, that the great human temptation is to regard an orientation as final and that succumbing leads to disaster," locates Hemingway's fear of history, his obsession with escaping war, the historical World War I, by recreating in environments of violence the components of his original terror.[9] In related manner, Montherlant's historical imagination, his continual evocation of the Romans, is only partially an attempt to fix history; it is also an attempt partially deriving from his fear that history will come again to overwhelm him. His entire work in whatever genre may be seen as an attempt to find his role, to assert a role, and in that assertion to avoid disaster.

In Malraux's work, the process is even more interesting than in either Hemingway's or Montherlant's. There is first the palpable fact that Malraux is inhumanly intelligent; his work is a splendid vindication of intelligence. He knows history, the philosophy of history, and his knowledge is everywhere reflected in his writing. His work is the supreme example of the uses of history in fiction, and an answer to the questions raised in this volume about the relationship of history to myth, to prose fiction. To this point I take a text from Nicola Chiaromonte: "When he described Fabrizio searching for the battle of Waterloo and not being able to find it, Stendhal was expressing, in his own nimble way, one of the great insights of nineteenth-century sensibility. It was a flash of pure wonder at the utterly paradoxical relation between an individual destiny and whatever general significance might be attached to a 'historical event.' In fact, it was the splendid illustration of a myth which no historical venture, and no amount of sophistry, has thereafter been able to obliterate from our consciousness." [10] The same is true, Chiaromonte says, of the "epic" moments of *War and Peace:* "The myth is about man and history: the more naïvely, and genuinely, man experiences a historical event, the more the event disappears, and something else takes its place: the starry sky, the other man, or the utterly ironical detail. That is, the unhistorical: Karataiev and his footgear appear infinitely more significant than Napoleon or Mother Russia. Yet man is inside the event as in a trap. History does not reveal its meaning, but gives way to destiny. We have the paradox of an irretrievable disproportion. For Stendhal, as for Tolstoy, the revelation brings with it an instant of catharsis. Something might or might not follow from it, but the moment of illumination and wonder has a value of its own, and can never be forgotten, or explained away: a stark question has been addressed by the living individual to the historical whirlwind, however mighty or majestic." [11]

This elegant and eloquent interpretation is assuredly valid for portions of Stendhal's work, and for all of *War and Peace;* it identifies the center of interest of both Stendhal and Tolstoy at the moments that Chiaromonte chooses to emphasize: namely, in the psychological. Malraux, however, is not a psychological writer, and readers (particularly in 1948, when Chiaromonte's essay was first published) are often ill-at-ease with fiction that is not written in the great, post-Romantic psychological convention. What Malraux does, I think, is the opposite of what Chiaromonte says that Stendhal and Tolstoy do. Malraux does not take us to nonexistent, mythical battles; he takes us to live revolutions and wars: to Canton province and to Shanghai in *Les Conquérants* and *La Condition humaine;* to the battlefronts of the Spanish Civil War, to actions in both world wars and the Turkish revolution in *Les Noyers de l'Altenburg.* That is to say, he goes to historical events, precisely, even minutely located in time and place. He then concentrates on the event rather than on the psychological reactions of his characters. The most intellectual of novelists, he is able to invent convincing characters, yet to avoid cluttering his historical and philosophical insights with attention to people's footgear, or to whether they have a cold in the head or an ache in the belly. How is that possible?

In order to answer the question, it is necessary that one examine Malraux's politics and the nature of the analysis of his work. The animus that one senses in Chiaromonte's essay, and one could cite many other such essays, is directed not so much against Malraux's conception of history as against Hegel's and Marx's. Malraux's Marxist coloration invites attack, particularly from those who, after 1945, were busy shedding their own prewar Marxist dress in favor of a suit of merely liberal cloth. Chiaromonte is of course correct in locating Malraux as an activist, but wrong, I think, in implying that for Malraux, action was an end in itself. Malraux was not Marxist, but apocalyptic, and insofar as Marxism may be regarded as apocalyptic, the two coincide. In both *Les Conquérants* of 1928 and *La Condition humaine* of 1933, the narratives are based upon Malraux's mysterious (in detail) activity during the mid-twenties as commissioner of propaganda for the revolutionary government of the South under the Communist Kuomintang.[12] Where *Les Conquérants* was concerned with the successful phase of the uprising, the second novel, with its title from Pascal, reverses the situation and presents the dissolution that followed the collapse of the Wuhan government and the brutal liquidation of the Left by the Kuomintang generals.

A triumph of construction and of craftsmanship, *La Condition humaine* is a cluster of brilliant images, each surrounded by aphoristic comments by one character to, or upon, the other, or upon the image itself. The images center on the characters, but those images are the carriers of an elucidated idea: Ch'en, whom we see first, and horribly, at the work of murdering a sleeping man, describes an image of the terrorist in revolution; he is identified only later as a man who despises affection and fears it, a man who would live, and die, by ideas. Kyo, the organizer of the Leftist group, lives for us as a man born to be betrayed, by his wife, by his distrust of the notion of political brotherhood, and by Clappique, the metaphysical tramp, who literally gambles away the hour in which his warning of disaster would have saved both Kyo and the revolutionary movement. Kyo is identified by his solitude: love does not free him from total solitude. He remarks that "in Marxism is a sense of a *fatalité* and the exaltation of will. Every time *fatalité* precedes will, I am suspicious." [13] Kyo thus places Nietzsche before Marx, an ordering of loyalties that is of course heresy for a Marxist. Gisors, Kyo's father, is the image of peace and contemplation; at first glance, he appears to represent for Malraux the still center amidst all the activity. He combines Buddhist passivity with Western intellectual propositions; he understands Ch'en's compulsion to act, but he also understands that Ch'en's "ideas had made him live; now they would kill him." [14] It slowly becomes clear to us, however, that Gisors's peace, his rationality, his tragic awareness, are at least partially the result of his addiction to opium. Drugs dislocate his senses, but no new world emerges; only awareness of apocalypse, and in the coda of the final chapter, defiance of apocalypse. He will go to Moscow,

with May, his dead son's unfaithful wife, to be professor in the
Sun Yat-sen Institute.

The center of the novel is neither in the image nor in the
character of Girsors; nor is it in the corrupt Clappique, nor in
Ferral, the colonialist manipulator; the center is in the figure
of Katow, as I read Malraux's intention. Katow is a hardened
revolutionary who fought against the White armies and
followed Kyo in his attempt to secure arms for continuing
opposition to the Kuomintang. After the failure of his group,
Katow lies among two hundred wounded, waiting to be
executed. He is put in an élite group of those who are not
simply shot, but are burned to death in the boiler of a locomotive. He meets Suan and a second, nameless terrorist, two
of those condemned for the attempt on Chiang Kai-shek's
life. The two terrorists are themselves terrified of death by
burning; Katow, who has a cyanide capsule, sufficient for
two, gives it to the two men: one a casual acquaintance, the
other unknown to him. He then goes to his own terrible
death, "le sifflet atroce" of the locomotive in his ears.[15] It
is a great scene, not in its action alone, although it is a tragic
action in the full sense of the term, but also in Katow's reflections on human dignity and on one's attempt, in spite of death,
to achieve human brotherhood. That complex of action and
reflection contains Malraux's meaning on the occasion when
he said to an interviewer that *la condition humaine*, human
destiny, is intolerable and to be denied. Katow denies, insofar
as man can deny, his own destiny, and in so doing commits a
noble suicide. Such an action transcends the Marxist notion of
class solidarity and takes on the "sense of an ending," in Frank
Kermode's fine phrase, beyond the apocalyptic to a super-
Apocalypse.

Malraux's characters are saintly rather than psychological;
one can therefore all the more readily agree with Trotsky that

the Malraux of *Les Conquérants* and *La Condition humaine* is not a Marxist, nor even a Trotskyite or Stalinist. For the orthodox, those novels (like the author himself) contained, in Trotsky's words, too much aesthetic caprice.[16] In his answer to Trotsky, Malraux provided a clue to how we might best read his fiction. He defended *Les Conquérants* against Trotsky's accusation that it is not an accurate reflection of the political revolution in China by writing that his novel was first of all "an accusation against the human condition." The word "accusation" is central; within the framework that it suggests, heroism, even tragedy, become possible. Second, Malraux found a splendid phrase to push aside excessive political interpretation: "L'optique du roman domine le roman": "the perspective of fiction dominates the novel." Third, and perhaps most important, Malraux wrote that Hong (the terrorist of *Les Conquérants*, prototype of Ch'en in the later novel) represents not the proletariat but *anarchy*. "His end is ethical, not political—and without hope." [17] In the heroes of his first two novels, Garine and Perken, too, one may find anarchy, that particular brand of anarchy deriving from Georges Sorel and his *Reflections on Violence*. Like his Existentialist critics, then, Malraux's Marxist critics are tempted by the nature of the material that fires his imagination—revolution, violence, war—to discover an ideological framework, which, if it is present, is not present precisely in the form such critics seek and require.

L'Espoir also has been interpreted as little more than a disorganized, hurried compilation of praise for the Loyalist armies in Spain; more often than not it has been read as a tract rather than as a novel. A generation after the event, perhaps we may more readily admit that here, too, "l'optique du roman domine le roman." In form, *L'Espoir* is virtually the reverse of *La Condition humaine*. It is loose, episodic, it contains many characters who are only sketched in, as op-

posed to the temporal and intellectual tightness of the earlier
novel. The scene is Madrid, Barcelona, Toledo, Guadala-
jara, all of Spain in fact; the protagonist is neither Garcia nor
Hernandez nor Ximenes, the characters we know most fully,
but revolution itself and its effects upon men in society.
Toward the end of the novel, Garcia, the propaganda officer
in the Loyalist force, is speaking to Scali, the Italian exile,
about men's motives in revolution. Their conversation is
valuable for what it tells us about Malraux's previous work,
and for its prophecy of the most important theme of *Les Noyers
de l'Altenburg* still to come. Garcia says,

"Intellectuals always tend to think that a political party is made up
of men united around an idea. A party is closer to a living character
than to an idea! To consider only the psychological aspect, a party
is really an organization for carrying out a common action, a nexus of
feelings often contradictory, such as poverty, humiliation, an apocalyptic conviction, hope. And where the Communists are concerned,
a taste for action, for organization, for production, and the like. To
deduce a man's psychology from his party's program would be the
same as my having tried to deduce the psychology of my Peruvians
from their religious myths, my dear friend." [18]

Garcia and Scali leave the building in which they have been
talking. It is under artillery fire, as is the entire inner city.
They speak of Unamuno and make tacit reference to *The Tragic
Sense of Life*.

"Unamuno will have died in the wrong place," Scali said. "Fate
had prepared for him here the funeral of his life-long dream."
Garcia thought of the room in Salamanca. [A reference to Unamuno's
house arrest for refusal to support the revolutionary forces against
the Loyalists.]
"He would have found another tragedy here," he said, "and I am
not sure that he would have understood it. The great intellectual is
the man of nuance, of degree, of quality, of truth for its own sake, of
complexity. By definition and in essence, anti-Manichean. Now, all

the ways of action are Manichean because *all action is Manichean.* It is most acutely so where the masses are involved, but it remains so even if it does not involve them. Every true revolutionary is a Manichean. And all politics." [P. 745.]

This seems to me an accurate reflection upon the meaning, political only in part, of all Malraux's allegedly political novels. His novels are not in stasis, but in flux; he displays those terrible and tragic moments when men move from flux to stasis, from life to death. He does so in intellectual terms, through intellectual spokesmen; but as Garcia's and Scali's conversation makes clear, Malraux distrusts the intellect, just as he has no illusions about the superiority of action over contemplation. Ideology does not determine man's virtue, Scali says, in effect, as the conversation, and the bombardment, go on. Formerly, to be a good man meant to be a good Christian. To be a good man is not necessarily to be a Communist. Garcia answers,

"The question is not inconsiderable, for it's the question of civilization itself, my good friend. For a time the learned man—let's call him the scholar—was considered pretty explicitly to be the superior European man. The intellectuals were the clergy of a world in which politicians, for better or worse, represented the aristocracy. That clergy was not challenged. It was the intellectuals, and not the others, Miguel [de Unamuno] and not Alfonso XIII, and for that matter, Miguel and not the Bishopric, whose task it was to teach men how to live. But here we are in a time when the new political leaders claim to rule our minds: Miguel against Franco (and against us until only yesterday), Thomas Mann against Hitler, Gide against Stalin, Ferrero against Mussolini: it is a Quarrel of Investitures." [P. 747.]

It is in this same dialogue that Malraux invents a justly famous exchange. Scali asks how one can make the best of one's life, and the answer, "Transformer en conscience une expérience aussi large que possible . . . (p. 748)." ("By converting

as wide a range of experience as possible into conscious
thought. . . .")

L'Espoir abounds in epigram and aphorism, as it abounds
in characters who represent all manner of approach to the
central, historical fact of revolution. Puig, the Catalan anarchist, at the moment of his death affirms against his anarchistic
ideology the possibility of victory. Ximenes, of the hated
Guardia Civil, who has spent his life in putting down upris-
ings (as his son still does), refuses to join the rebels under
Franco and puts his skill and training to work as a commander
of the Loyalists, all the while remaining ardently Catholic
and largely human before the attacks of the young ideologists
in his command. We find heroes in *L'Espoir*, as in the other
novels, but no hero, no central character. Heroic acts in turn,
in the early work, tend to appear solipsistic; we have seen
Malraux define them as anarchistic. When Kyo, in *La Condition humaine*, appears to be taking on traditional heroic garments, he disappears from sight, and still another agonist—
Katow, or Hemelrich—turns up. Kassner, in *Les Jours du
mépris*, might seem the exception, since his narrative does
dominate, yet one wonders. The protagonist, one is forced
to conclude, is history itself, or rather an irrational affirmation
about man before the backdrop of history that dominates all
Malraux's fiction, and indeed all the published work of his
maturity.

Malraux himself supports that view, for whatever his support may be worth. (One reads writers' comments on their own
work with suspicion.) When his neglect of the personal voice
in his characters was questioned, Malraux responded,

I wonder if in your analysis there is not a notion of the specific
nature of the novel, a notion that has always been suspect to me.
.   .   .   .

The autonomy of characters, the particular vocabulary given to
each of them, are powerful techniques of fictional action; they are

not necessities. They are more evident in *Gone with the Wind* than in *The Possessed*, and nonexistent in *Adolphe*. I do not believe that the novelist must create characters; he must create a particular and coherent world, just like any other artist. He should not compete with the world of vital statistics, but with the reality that is imposed on him, the reality of "life," seeming at times to submit to it, and at other times to transform it, in order to rival life.[19]

Malraux points out the silliness of much of the dialogue in Balzac, and the absence of individualized dialogue in Dostoevsky. He continues,

The more convincing the hero of a novel, the more convincing his life, which is not quite like that of other men. The potency of fictional illusion is not always born from the writer's ability to endow his characters with independent existence, transmitted as such. I believe that for a large number of novelists and playwrights, the characters grow out of the drama, not the drama out of the characters; the heroes of Aeschylus, as well as those of Shakespeare, of Dostoevsky and Stendhal, are the "projections" of their authors, around whom, like the objects in certain surrealist paintings, a *trompe-l'œil* mob assembles or scatters.[20]

Here we have moved beyond mere absence of psychology in Malraux's characters to a Shakespearean projection of meaning as lying between the event and that understanding of character we may achieve from seeing the fictional character involved in the event. We are at the mysterious center at which fiction becomes knowledge, fiction transmits knowledge. Knowledge of the event, whether given in the fictional account or whether residing in our minds from previous knowledge, provides either a background or a foreground for our ultimate knowledge that is the product of the movement (or in the Aristotelean sense, the action) of character. That knowledge is not syllogistic; it is finally intuitive and emotional. Malraux's characters, accordingly, may be seen as a horde of Iagos, characters inexplicable at the merely psychological level; and Malraux's action then can be interpreted not in the dramatic terms of Othello's jealousy, but in terms of the novelist's concern for the human pattern resulting from a historical confrontation with what he calls *fatalité*.

Les Noyers de l'Altenburg clarifies much of this matter, for among other things, it is a prolonged debate on the subject of the philosophy of history, as well as a moving presentation of three layers of historical movement: World War I, the Turkish uprising, and World War II. The war setting is important, for it again shows us Malraux going to a basic Romantic preoccupation: the contemplation of man's reactions when he is stripped of culture, stripped by events of the defenses that we call civilization. The narrative begins after the fall of France, in 1940, with the narrator reflecting in a prisoner-of-war compound upon the fact that he is seeing man in essence, man in his primeval state. In the second section, we find the experience of the narrator's father, Vincent Berger, in Asia, his return to Europe, after many years' absence, and his mystical apprehension, upon his arrival, that man is indeed free, that about his existence is a quality of the sacred. What that quality is or may be is the substance of the long portion of the novel given over to the debate at Altenburg, a debate in which the answer to Vincent Berger's question is provided, although in conspicuously sibylline fashion.

Möllberg, the quasi-Spengler-cum-Frobenius,[21] sees man as locked in his historical epoch and therefore doomed. Vincent Berger speaks for the continuity of the human spirit in the face of Möllberg's historicism. For Möllberg, human life, insofar as it attempts to escape from the immediately given, is absurd and irrational. The key passage in the debate begins with the quotation about the "fundamental" previously quoted. One must pursue Malraux's course from that point. Möllberg maintains that the idea of fundamental man is a

myth of sentimental intellectuals about peasants of whom
intellectuals have no experience. To explain his point, he
refers to Walter Berger's passion for the walnut trees and for
the statues made from them at Altenburg. Möllberg maintains
that there is no such thing, however, as a fundamental *noyer*,
only a log. The only truth is animal:

> "Remove the capacity to reason, and you have sometimes a dog,
> sometimes a tiger, or a lion if you wish, but always an animal. All
> men eat, drink, sleep, and fornicate, to be sure; but they do not eat
> the same things, they do not drink the same things, they do not dream
> the same things. They have scarcely anything in common except to
> sleep when they sleep without dreams — and be dead." [22]

Rabaud answers by saying that surely in man there is
something of the divine, something eternal. Stieglitz affirms
the continuity of "the great Hegelian line"; the process of
integrating into the World Spirit new aspects of mind goes on,
creating not *one* history but a German history, a national history formed of elements previously heterogeneous. Möllberg agrees, saying that the Hegelian process backs up his
own view of man irrevocably caught up in one culture. His
experience of Africa, primitive, savage, outside history as he
understands it, is his ultimate answer.

After the debate, Vincent Berger goes into the garden,
where in a passage unusual in Malraux's work for its elicit-
ing of extraordinary natural beauty, Berger reflects on Möllberg's words about the statues, about the trees themselves, the
trees well-cultivated, so planted as best to frame the cathedral of Strasbourg in the distance. In the beauty of the trees
and the civilization that they symbolize lies Berger's answer
to Möllberg's destructive historicism: " 'Civilization or the
animal, statue versus log.' Between the statues and the logs

were the trees, their patterns as obscure as that of life"
(p. 106).

It is a peculiar answer for Malraux to have made, because
it is an American answer; it is the answer of Faulkner and
Hemingway, if not of Emerson and Thoreau. It is, in brief,
the transcendental answer rather than the Marxist or the
Existentialist answer. Throughout his fiction, Malraux has
moved from Byronic anarchy, from negative Romanticism, to
affirmation; almost, one is tempted to write, to redemption.
Of course it is not redemption, for in Berger's narrative, war
follows, and we live on, with our wars and revolutions, very
sadly in the post-Romantic era. Redemption is not for Berger, not for Malraux, nor, probably, for us.

I owe much to Morse Peckham; therefore let me owe a bit
more with a final quotation from him. His meaning is close
indeed to my meaning throughout the preceding pages:
"modern art is the triumph of Romanticism, that modern
culture, in its vital areas, is a Romantic culture, and . . .
nothing has yet replaced it. Since the logic of Romanticism
is that contradictions must be included in a single orientation,
but without pseudo-reconciliations, Romanticism is a remarkably stable and fruitful orientation. For the past 165 years the
Romantic has been the tough-minded man, determined to
create value and project order to make feasible the pure
assertion of identity, determined to assert identity in order
to engage with reality simply because it is there and because there is nothing else, and knowing eventually that his
orientations are adaptive instruments and that no orientation
is or can be final. The Romantic artist does not escape from
reality; he escapes into it." [23]

It is entirely possible that Romanticism, fully acknowledged and properly defined, may be our single hope for the

future of art, if art is to have a future. In a time of irrationality, of hostility to ideas in the degree that people in desperation will accept anything on its own terms, the various post-Romantic writers provide examples of how we may use our rationality without adopting the attitude of the neo-Neoclassicist. The variety of knowledge that we derive from the art form of the novel will not serve us in the daily world of getting and spending; it is not the business of art to give answers. The particular order of knowledge that we discover in the visions of history of our best novelists suggests that rationality and intuition, as used by the Romantics, both historical and contemporary, are not to be despised, but to be honored and possibly even imitated.

Notes

Notes to *Preliminaries*

1. *New Literary History* published an entire issue on the question, "Is Literary History Obsolete?" II, no. 1 (Autumn, 1970). A significant number of contributors, although with appropriate reservations, answered in the affirmative. René Wellek, "The Attack on Literature," *The American Scholar*, XLII, no. 1 (Winter, 1972–73), 27–42, is a wholesome rebuttal of that affirmative.
2. Friedrich Nietzsche, *Werke*, ed. Karl Schlechta, 3 vols. (Munich: Carl Hanser, 1960), II, 1111.
3. Maurice Blanchot is quoted in Gaëtan Picon, *Malraux par lui-même* (Paris: Editions du Seuil, 1963), p. 186.
4. A. O. Lovejoy, "On the Discrimination of Romanticisms," *PMLA*, XXIX (1924), 228–253.
5. Jacques Barzun, *Classic, Romantic and Modern* (London: Secker and Warburg, 1962); previously published as *Romanticism and the Modern Ego* (1943). René Wellek, "The Concept of Romanticism in Literary History," *Comparative Literature*, I, no. 1 (1949), 1–23; I, no. 2 (1949), 147–172.
6. Such is emphatically not the case in German scholarship and criticism. The Germans have always been far more precise about Romanticism than the other Europeans, including the English, or the Americans. A recent and welcome example is: Wolfgang Paulsen, ed., *Das Nachleben der Romantik* (Heidelberg: Lothar Stiehm, 1968).
7. Richard Ellmann and Charles Feidelson, Jr., eds., *The Modern Tradition: Backgrounds of Modern Literature* (New York: Oxford University Press, 1965).
8. T. S. Eliot, "Shelley and Keats," in *The Use of Poetry and the Use of Criticism* (London: Faber and Faber, 1933), p. 100.
9. *Ibid.*, p. 91.
10. Ernest Lee Tuveson, *The Imagination as a Means of Grace: Locke and the Aesthetics of Romanticism* (Berkeley: University of California Press, 1960), p. 26.
11. Jacques Rivière is cited in Tuveson, p. 175.

12. *Novalis Werke,* ed. Gerhard Schulz (Munich: C. H. Beck, 1969), p. 493.

13. Barzun, pp. 58–61. Barzun does not cite Novalis to the point, but he might have quoted paragraphs 17 and 18 of the *Allgemeinen Brouillon:*

(17) "ROMANTICISM. To reach for the absolute, the universal—the *classification* of individual moments [of being], of the individual situation, etc., is the characteristic mode of the Romantic. See Wilhelm Meister. Fairy-tales."

(18) "How few people possess the *genius* to experiment. The true experimenter must have a *dark feeling for Nature* within himself, to the degree that the more perfect his plans, the more compellingly he will follow his instincts, and with great *precision* discover the hidden, essential phenomena and reveal them as though destined to do so. Nature, as it were, inspires the true admirer and reveals itself in proportion to the harmony of his constitution with Nature. The true lover of Nature reveals himself through his readiness to multiply his experiments, to simplify, to combine and to analyze, to romanticize and to popularize, through his appetite for ever newer experiments. He reveals himself through his natural taste and sensitivity in selection and arrangement, through the acuteness and clarity of his observations, and in his descriptions of his observations. Further, the experimenter is, simply, the Genius." *Novalis Werke,* p. 452. Novalis' emphasis; my translation.

14. Barzun, pp. 97–102.

Notes to Chapter 1: *Romanticism and Modern Fiction: Proust*

1. Friedrich Nietzsche, *Aus dem Nachlass der Achtzigerjahre,* in *Werke,* ed. Karl Schlechta, 3 vols. (Munich: Hanser, 1960), III, 496.

2. Max Harold Fisch, "Introduction," *The Autobiography of Giambattista Vico,* trans. Max Harold Fisch and Thomas Goddard Bergin (Ithaca, N.Y.: Cornell University Press, 1963), pp. 67–68.

3. *Novalis Werke,* ed. Gerhard Schulz (Munich: C. H. Beck, 1969), p. 499. Novalis' emphasis.

4. *Ibid.*, p. 498.
5. *Ibid.*, p. 357.
6. *Ibid.*, p. 358. Novalis' emphasis on uniforms evokes Hermann Broch's Joachim von Pasenow, in vol. I of *Die Schlafwandler,* who fears personal disintegration should he remove his uniform.
7. *Novalis Werke,* pp. 535–536.
8. *Ibid.*, p. 454.
9. Paul Kluckhohn, "Die romantische Staatsauffassung bei Novalis," in *Novalis: Beiträge zu Werk und Persönlichkeit Friedrich von Hardenbergs,* ed. Gerhard Schulz (Darmstadt: Wissenschaftliche Buchgesellschaft, 1970), pp. 98–104. Hans Wolfgang Kuhn gives an existentialist gloss to Novalis' politics in *Der Apokalyptiker und die Politik* (Freiburg im Breisgau: Rombach: 1961).
10. *Novalis Werke,* pp. 405–406.
11. *Ibid.*, p. 565.
12. Hans Kohn, *The Mind of Germany* (London: Macmillan, 1961), pp. 63–64. Also, Adam Müller, *Die Elemente der Staatskunst: Sechsunddreissig Vorlesungen* (Meersburg am Bodensee and Leipzig: Hendel, 1936), pp. 390–392; Nachwort, p. 438, passim. "Nations (Völker) and laws are always and everywhere formed interdependently; if they are separated, both the will of the people and the benefits of law are negated. Deprived of some manner of national form, the work of the lawmakers and the writers of constitutions means nothing, just as the private efforts and private formation of a people also come to nothing" (p. 438).
13. A part of Hegel's monstrosity lies in the obscurity of his prose, which defies literal translation. The rendering here is as literal as is consistent with communication. Hegel's original German is given here and in the notes that follow: "Zuerst müssen wir beachten, dass unser Gegenstand, die *Weltgeschichte,* auf dem geistigen Boden vorgeht. Welt begreift die psychische und physische Natur in sich; die physische Natur greift gleichfalls in die Weltgeschichte ein, und wir werden schon im Anfange aud diese Grundverhältnisse der Naturbestimmung aufmerksam machen. Aber der Geist und der Verlauf seiner Entwicklung ist das Substantielle. Die Natur haben wir hier nicht zu betrachten, wie sie an ihr selbst gleichfalls ein System der Vernunft ist, in

einem besonderen, eigentümlichen Elemente, sondern nur relativ auf den Geist." G. W. F. Hegel, *Werke,* ed. Eva Moldenhauer and Karl Markus Michel (Frankfurt-am-Main: Suhrkamp, 1970), XII, 29.

14. I follow Karl Löwith's reading of Hegel here, to which I am indebted. *From Nietzsche to Hegel* (London: Constable, 1964), p. 208.

15. "Eine philosophische Eintheilung ist überhaupt nicht eine aüsserliche, nach irgend einem oder mehreren aufgenommenen Eintheilungsgründen gemachte aüssere Klassifierung eines vorhandenen Stoffes, sondern das immanente Unterscheiden des Begriffes selbst." G. W. F. Hegel, *Sämtliche Werke,* ed. Hermann Glockner (Stuttgart: Fr. Frommans, 1952), VII, 85. John M. E. McTaggart's critique is to the point, in "The Relation of the Dialectic to Time," Chap. 5 of *Studies in the Hegelian Dialectic* (Cambridge: 1922), pp. 157–200.

16. "Indem wir es also nur mit der Idee des Geistes zu thun haben, und in der Weltgeschichte Alles nur als seine Erscheinung betrachten, so haben wir die Vergangenheit, wie gross sie auch immer sei, durchlaufen, es nur mit Gegenwärtigem zu thun; denn die Philosophie, als sich mit dem Wahren beschäftigend, hat es mit ewig Gegenwärtigem zu thun. Alles ist ihr in der Vergangenheit unverloren, denn die Idee ist präsent, der Geist unsterblich d.h. er ist nicht vorbei und ist nicht noch nicht, sondern ist wesentlich isst. So ist hiemit schon gesagt, dass die gegenwärtige Gestalt des Geistes alle früheren Stufen in sich begreift." Hegel, *Sämtliche Werke; Philosophie der Geschichte,* II, 119–120.

17. Löwith, p. 215.

18. Wilhelm Dilthey, *Gesammelte Schriften* (Göttingen: Vandenhoeck und Ruprecht, 1958), VII, 207. Trans. J. J. Kuehl, in *Theories of History,* ed. Patrick Gardner (New York: Free Press, 1959), pp. 213–225.

19. Dilthey, *Gesammelte Schriften,* VII, 208. Kuehl's translation.

20. *Ibid.,* pp. 212–213. And see H. A. Hodges, *The Philosophy of Wilhelm Dilthey* (London: Routledge and Kegan Paul, 1952), pp. 275–277.

21. Proust's complex techniques of narration have been widely

analyzed: e.g., Louis Martin-Chauffier, "Proust and the Double I," *Partisan Review* (October, 1949), 1011–1026; and B. G. Rogers, *Proust's Narrative Techniques* (Geneva: Droz, 1965).

22. And as in Barrès' fiction. Walter A. Strauss, *Proust and Literature* (Cambridge, Mass.: Harvard University Press, 1957), p. 216.

23. Marcel Proust, *Remembrance of Things Past*, trans. C. K. Scott Moncrieff (New York: Random House, 1934), I, 141. *À la recherche du temps perdu*, Bibliothèque de la Pléiade (Paris: Gallimard, 1954), I, 183–184.

24. *À la recherche* . . . , I, 184. My emphasis and my translation. Scott Moncrieff translates "C'est parce que je croyais aux choses" "It is because I used to *think* of certain things. . . ." A mistranslation of Proust's intention in the verb "croire" if I read him correctly.

25. Joseph Frank, "Spatial Form in Modern Literature," in *The Widening Gyre* (New Brunswick, N.J.: Rutgers University Press, 1963), pp. 3–62.

26. Arnaldo Momigliano notes that A. O. Lovejoy traced how Bergson developed ideas of the German Romantic philosophers. Momigliano, "Time in Ancient Historiography," in *History and the Concept of Time* (Middletown, Conn.: Wesleyan University Press, 1966), p. 4. Proust, a cousin through marriage of Bergson, knew Bergson's teachings and attended his lectures at the Sorbonne. George D. Painter, *Marcel Proust: A Biography* (London: Vol. I, 1959; Vol. II, 1965), I, 80.

27. Proust, *À la recherche* . . . , III, 723–724. *Time Regained*, trans. Andreas Mayor (London: Chatto and Windus, 1970), pp. 33–36. Page numbers following texts subsequently quoted refer to these editions. Mayor's translation of the final volume must be preferred, for it reflects the scholarly work on the French text as incorporated in the Pléiade edition.

28. Proust, *Time Regained*, p. 50. *À la recherche* . . . , III, 735.

29. Proust, *Time Regained*, p. 57. *À la recherche* . . . , III, 741.

30. Proust, *Time Regained*, p. 71. *À la recherche* . . . , III, 751.

31. "There may be a connection between the development of tragedy and the development of historiography in the fifth century [B.C.]." Momigliano, "Time in Ancient Historiography," p. 10, and notes.

Notes to Chapter 2: *Hermann Broch*

1. Georg Lukács' *Der historische Roman* was first published in Moscow, translated from German, 1937. First (East) German edition, 1955; (West) German edition, 1961. English translation, Hannah and Stanley Mitchell (London: Merlin Press, 1962). References are to the Beacon paperback edition, *The Historical Novel* (Boston, 1963).
2. Lukács, *The Historical Novel*, pp. 28–29.
3. *Ibid.*, p. 25.
4. *Ibid.*, pp. 273, 275.
5. "Man is what has happened to him, what he has done.
   "In sum, man does not possess naturalness, what he possesses is history." José Ortega y Gasset, *Historia como sistema* (Madrid: Occidente, 1942), p. 63. My translation.
6. Miguel de Unamuno, Introduction to *La agonía del cristianismo,* in another version of the idea: "In contrast to physical, corporeal life, the psychic or spiritual life is a struggle against the oblivion of eternity; and against history, because history, which is God's thinking in the land of men, is lacking in ultimate humanity. It is the road to oblivion, to inconsequence. All man's effort is to give human finality to history, superhuman finality, as Nietzsche would have said, he who was the great trumpeter of the absurd. . . ." *Obras completas*, IV (Madrid: Aguado, 1950), 830–831. My translation.
7. Trevelyan is quoted in Jacques Barzun, *Classic, Romantic and Modern* (London: Secker and Warburg, 1962), p. 61.
8. Lukács, *The Historical Novel*, p. 62.
9. *Ibid.*, p. 33. And see p. 34. For a cogent critique of *The Historical Novel*, see Ursula Brumm, "Thoughts on History and the Novel," *Comparative Literature Studies*, VI, no. 3 (1969), 317–330.
10. Hermann Broch, *Briefe von 1929 bis 1951*, ed. Robert Pick (Zurich: Rhein-Verlag, 1957), p. 321. Vol. VIII of *Gesammelte Werke*, in 10 volumes; hereafter cited as *Werke*.
11. R. P. Blackmur, *Eleven Essays in the European Novel* (New York: Harcourt, Brace and World, 1964), pp. 30–31.
12. Manfred Durzak, *Hermann Broch: Der Dichter und seine Zeit* (Stuttgart: Kohlhammer, 1968), p. 18.

13. By Hannah Arendt *et al.*, *Dichter wider Willen: Einführung in das Werk von Hermann Broch* (Zurich: Rhein-Verlag, 1958), pp. 41–46. Reprinted in Broch, *Werke*, VI, 5 ff.

14. Broch, *Werke*, VI, 9.

15. *Ibid.*, p. 263. The quotation is from Broch's introduction to Rachel Bespaloff's *Iliad*, which Broch wrote in English. His use of the word "poetry" suggests that he had in mind the untranslatable German word *Dichtung*, which can mean both "poetry" and "prose."

16. See Durzak, pp. 16–18, for Broch's neo-Kantian study.

17. On Broch's Platonism, see Ernestine Schlant, *Die Philosophie Hermann Brochs* (Bern and Munich: Francke, 1971), pp. 10–11, passim. Also Durzak, pp. 26–30.

18. "Anyone who is satisfied with subjective interjections is no artist, he is no poet; self-knowledge is nothing. Intuitive knowledge is everything." In "Hofmannsthal und seine Zeit," *Broch, Werke*, VI, 152.

19. *Ibid.*, p. 237.

20. *Ibid.*, p. 184.

21. *Ibid.*, p. 195

22. *Ibid.*, p. 201.

23. *Ibid.*, p. 204.

24. *Ibid.*, VIII, 60. Broch's emphasis.

25. For Broch's attention to historical dates, see Heinz D. Osterle, "Hermann Broch, *Die Schlafwandler:* Revolution and Apocalypse," *PMLA*, LXXXVI, no. 5 (1971), 946–949.

26. Osterle's word, in his impressive article on Broch's political intent. *Ibid.*, p. 955.

27. Broch, *Die Schlafwandler, Werke*, II, 14. *The Sleepwalkers*, trans. Willa and Edwin Muir (New York: Pantheon, 1947), pp. 15–16. Further citations in the text are to the translation.

28. Morse Peckham, "Toward a Theory of Romanticism," *PMLA*, LXVI, no. 2 (1951), 15.

29. *Ibid.*, p. 20.

30. Morse Peckham, "Toward a Theory of Romanticism: II. Reconsiderations," *Studies in Romanticism*, I, no. 1 (Autumn, 1961), 5. Peckham's articles on Romanticism have been collected in *The Triumph of Romanticism* (Columbia: University of South Carolina Press, 1970).

31. G. C. Schoolfield, "Broch's Sleepwalkers: Aeneas and the Apostles," *The James Joyce Review*, II, no. 2 (Spring-Summer, 1958), 21–38.
32. Some of the ideas and some of the language in Chapter II first appeared in John McCormick, "James Joyce and Hermann Broch: From Influence to Originality," *Proceedings of the IVth Congress of the International Comparative Literature Association* (The Hague, Paris: Mouton, 1966), pp. 1344–1352.

Notes to Chapter 3: *Robert Musil*

1. Robert Musil, *The Man without Qualities*, trans. Eithne Wilkins and Ernst Kaiser, 3 volumes (London: Secker and Warburg, 1953, 1954, 1960). We know from Musil's published journals and letters that he planned his novel as a single entity, but that it was to appear in two volumes of four parts. The English translation includes only thirty-eight chapters of Musil's third part; some 552 pages of the German edition have not been translated, owing in part to the textual difficulties alluded to in my text. Musil's *Gesammelte Werke* is in three volumes: ed. Adolfe Frisé (Hamburg: Rowohlt), *Der Mann ohne Eigenschaften* (1952); *Tagebücher, Aphorismen, Essays und Reden* (1955); *Prosa, Dramen, späte Briefe* (1957).
2. Ernst Kaiser and Eithne Wilkins, *Robert Musil: Eine Einführung in das Werk* (Stuttgart: Kohlhammer, 1962), p. 24.
3. Frisé's account of the textual problem is in the Rowohlt edition of *Der Mann ohne Eigenschaften*, pp. 1657–1663. Wilhelm Bausinger, *Studien zu einer historisch-kritischen Ausgabe von Robert Musils "Der Mann ohne Eigenschaften"* (Hamburg: Rowohlt, 1964), attacks Frisé's editorial work at great length and with authority. For a statement of the editorial problem as of 1970, see Dietrich Uffhausen, "Einige Bemerkungen zur Edition einer historisch-kritischen Ausgabe von Robert Musils Roman *Der Mann ohne Eigenschaften*," in Karl Dinklage, ed., *Robert Musil: Studien zu seinem Werk* (Hamburg: Rowohlt, 1970), pp. 371–410.
4. By Kaiser and Wilkins, *Eine Einführung*, p. 24.

5. Musil, *Tagebücher*, p. 572. And see Peter Nusser, *Musils Roman-theorie* (The Hague, Paris: Mouton, 1967), pp. 33–37.
6. Page references are to the Rowohlt edition and to the Kaiser and Wilkins translation, cited above.
7. See paragraph 36, Roman Ingarden, *Das literarische Kunstwerk* (Tübingen: Niemeyer, 1965).
8. Michael Hamburger, *From Prophecy to Exorcism* (London: Longmans, 1965), p. 97.
9. This notion has been interestingly studied by Manfred Sera, *Utopie und Parodie* (Bonn: H. Bouvier, 1969).
10. Musil entitled early fragments of his novel *Die Zwillingsch-wester* (The Twins); also *Der Spion* (The Spy), and *Der Erlöser* (The Redeemer).
11. Hamburger, *From Prophecy to Exorcism*, p. 96.
12. See Chapter II above, pp. 55 ff.
13. See Erhard von Büren, *Zur Bedeutung der Psychologie in Werk Robert Musils* (Zürich and Freiburg: Atlantis, 1970), and Bibli-ography. Also "More on Musil," *Times Literary Supplement* (27 September 1963), 752.
14. R. G. Collingwood, *The Idea of History* (London, New York: Oxford University Press, 1946; rptd. 1968), p. 15.

Notes to Chapter 4: *William Faulkner, the Past, and History*

1. Thanks to the Nazis and to World War II, neither Musil nor Broch was known to more than a handful of German readers as late as the mid-1950's.
2. "Der Historiker muss im Vortrag oft Redner werden—Er trägt ja *Evangelien* vor, denn die ganze Geschichte ist Evangelium." *Novalis Werke*, ed. Gerhard Schulz (Munich: C. H. Beck, 1969), p. 537.
3. Introduction to Marcel Raymond, *From Baudelaire to Surreal-ism* (New York: Wittenborn, Schultz, 1950), n.p. This is from Rosenberg's early, John the Baptist period, when he was just at the edge of the wilderness of anti-art.
4. *Faulkner: A Collection of Critical Essays*, ed. Robert Penn Warren (Englewood Cliffs, N.J.: Prentice-Hall, 1966), p. 295.

5. *Ibid.*, p. 274.
6. Jean-Paul Sartre, "Time in Faulkner: *The Sound and the Fury*," in *William Faulkner: Three Decades of Criticism*, ed. Frederick J. Hoffman and Olga W. Vickery (E. Lansing, Mich.: Michigan State University Press, 1960), pp. 229–230. Sartre's emphasis.
7. William Faulkner, *Intruder in the Dust* (New York: Random House, 1948), pp. 194–195.
8. Robert Penn Warren, "Introduction: Faulkner: Past and Future," in *Faulkner: A Collection of Critical Essays*, pp. 2–4.
9. Some of the above material derives from my discussion of Faulkner in *The Middle Distance* (New York: Macmillan Free Press, 1971), pp. 98–106.
10. William Faulkner, *Light in August* (New York: Harrison Smith and Robert Haas, 1932), p. 156.

Notes to Chapter 5: *The Anachronous Hero:
Hemingway and Montherlant*

1. Leon Edel, "The Art of Evasion," in *Hemingway: A Collection of Critical Essays*, ed. R. P. Weeks (Englewood Cliffs, N.J.: Prentice-Hall, 1962), pp. 169–170.
2. Ernest Hemingway, *The Fifth Column and the First Forty-nine Stories* (New York: Scribner's, 1938), pp. 243–244.
3. Ernest Hemingway, *The Sun Also Rises* (New York: Scribner's, 1954), p. 93.
4. Anonymous reviewer quoted in José Luis Castillo-Puche, *Hemingway entre la vida y la muerte* (Barcelona, 1968), p. 359.
5. Henry de Montherlant, *Romans et œuvres de fiction non théâtrales*, Bibliothèque de la Pléiade (Paris: Gallimard, 1962), p. 166. Further references are to this edition. My translations.
6. Some of the matter on Hemingway and Montherlant appeared in different form in "The Romantic Warriors," Chapter 4, in my book *The Middle Distance* (New York: Macmillan/Free Press, 1971).
7. In three essays on Barrès, Montherlant acknowledged an intellectual debt to Barrès but denied direct literary influence. See *Essais*, Bibliothèque de la Pléiade (Paris: Gallimard, 1963), pp. 265–285. Montherlant often quotes Nietzsche in his essays

and journals. There is undoubtedly a strain of D'Annunzio, too, in Montherlant's combination of egotism and eroticism. He wrote that he read D'Annunzio in the French translation of Georges Hérelle, and that his youthful works, including *Le Songe,* were influenced accordingly. Unpublished letter to Mr. L. Spitalnick, 10 May 1966. In March, 1963, Montherlant published an article, "Hommage à d'Annunzio," in which he wrote that before reading *Il Fuoco* in 1915, he had been a "prisoner of Flaubert, but that D'Annunzio untied the cords." Again, "My first two books, *La Relève du matin* and *Le Songe* are full of *Il Fuoco* to the point of intoxication."

8. Thus the title of Montherlant's volume of essays of 1935, *Service inutile.*

9. See Montherlant's essay "Syncrétisme et alternance" (1925), in *Essais,* pp. 237–245. Emerson was well known in France to men of Montherlant's generation (and earlier; to Proust, e.g.). It is likely that Montherlant had read Emerson. On syncretism in the nineteenth century, see Morse Peckham, *Beyond the Tragic Vision* (New York: Braziller 1962), pp. 264–265.

10. In the avant-propos to *La Rose de sable* (Paris: Gallimard, 1968), Montherlant said that he wrote the novel between 1930 and 1932, in Algeria and Paris. Fearing loss of his manuscript in the war obviously to come, Montherlant in 1938 caused sixty-five copies of the novel, entitled *Mission providentielle* under the pseudonym François Lazerge, to be printed and distributed to friends for safekeeping. In 1954, Plon published a long fragment, *L'Histoire d'amour de "La Rose de sable."* A limited edition of the final text was published by Lefebvre in 1967.

11. A case for Hemingway's play, *The Fifth Column,* might be made, but that play fails as a play through Hemingway's inadequacy when he tackles history head-on, in contrast to such a writer as André Malraux.

12. Avant-propos, *La Rose de sable,* p. x.

13. *Ibid.,* p. xi.

14. Emil Staiger, *Geist und Zeitgeist* (Zürich and Freiburg: Atlantis, 1964, 1969), p. 19.

15. Delmore Schwartz wrote of Hemingway that in the perspective of the past, he was most like Jane Austen, "who was very much interested in a special kind of conduct. . . . She also used con-

versation for the sake of a kind of rhetoric." "Ernest Hemingway's Literary Situation," in John K. McCaffery, ed., *Ernest
Hemingway: The Man and His Work* (Cleveland and New York:
World, 1950), p. 117. I have said that "The idea of comparing
the creator of Mr. Knightley with the creator of Count Mippipo-
polous may be shocking," but it indicates another context in
which to contrast Montherlant and the American writer.

Notes to Chapter 6: *André Malraux*

1. Léon Trotsky, "La Révolution étranglée," *La Nouvelle Revue
   Française*, No. 211 (1 April 1931), 489.
2. Joseph Frank, in "André Malraux: The Image of Man," wrote
   that ". . . Existentialist themes were given unforgettable artistic
   expression by Malraux long before they became fashionable
   intellectual catchwords or tedious artistic platitudes. Indeed,
   the genesis of French Existentialism as a full-fledged cultural
   movement probably owes more to Malraux than to Heidegger
   or Jaspers, Berdyaev or Chestov. For it was Malraux, through
   his novels, who shaped the sensibilities that then seized on doc-
   trinal Existentialism as an ideological prop." *The Widening
   Gyre* (New Brunswick, N.J.: Rutgers University Press, 1963),
   p. 106.
3. Jeanne Delhomme, Epigraph, *Temps et destin: Essai sur André
   Malraux* (Paris: Gallimard, 1955), n.p.
4. Mlle Delhomme's epigraph concludes: "In a reflection on
   original destiny which is the true [meaning of] time, the interrogation formulates itself, explains itself and transcends itself,
   because it is time, not empirical time successive and always on
   the move, history and chance, but that time which works of art
   name as their common profundity that is the horizon of the fundamental; it is then time, subterranean and nocturnal power
   which, in man, surpasses man, which engenders the metaphysical
   interrogation, sustains it, runs the risk of destroying it, retains it
   and consumes it in the dimension of the eternal return." My
   (very literal) translation.
5. See note 2, above.

6. I agree with Denis Boak, *André Malraux* (Oxford: Clarendon Press, 1968), p. 24, passim, regarding Nietzschean influence on Malraux.
7. Morse Peckham, "Toward a Theory of Romanticism," *PMLA,* LXVI, no. 2 (1951), 20.
8. Morse Peckham, "Toward a Theory of Romanticism, II: Reconsiderations," *Studies in Romanticism,* I, no. 1 (Autumn, 1961), 1–8.
9. An earlier American, Ralph Waldo Emerson, was also accused of resisting history and of conceiving of reality itself as "ultimately a-historical. That this course of thought involves the reduction of history to an illusion and experience to a pin-point present, and finally to the obliteration of the distinction between contingent and absolute Being, Emerson is well aware. . . ." A. Robert Caponigri, "Browning and Emerson: Nature and History," *New England Quarterly,* XVIII (1945), 371.
10. Nicola Chiaromonte, "Malraux and the Demons of Action," in *Malraux: A Collection of Critical Essays,* ed. R. W. B. Lewis (Englewood Cliffs, N.J.: Prentice-Hall, 1964), p. 98.
11. *Ibid.,* pp. 98–99.
12. Anon., "André Malraux," *The Observer* (London) (7 March 1954).
13. André Malraux, *Romans,* Bibliothèque de la Pléiade (Paris: Gallimard, 1947), p. 265. My translations.
14. *Ibid.,* p. 208.
15. *Ibid.,* p. 392.
16. See note 1, above.
17. André Malraux, "Réponse à Léon Trotsky," *La Nouvelle Revue Française,* no. 211 (1 April 1931), 502–505.
18. Malraux, *Romans,* pp. 744–745.
19. Gaëtan Picon, *Malraux par lui-même* (Paris: Editions du Seuil, 1963), p. 38.
20. *Ibid.,* p. 41.
21. Boak, pp. 158–161, traces Malraux's primary debt to Frobenius, and his only secondary debt to Spengler, for Möllberg's views.
22. André Malraux, *La Lutte avec l'ange* (*Les Noyers de l'Altenburg*) (Geneva: Albert Skira, 1943), p. 102.
23. Peckham, "Toward a Theory of Romanticism, II: Reconsiderations," p. 8.

Index